KYRIE IRVING

KYRIE IRVING

Uncle Drew, Little Mountain, and Enigmatic NBA Superstar

MARTIN GITLIN

UNIVERSITY OF NEBRASKA PRESS | LINCOLN

Library of Congress Cataloging-in-Publication Data
Names: Gitlin, Marty, author.
Title: Kyrie Irving: Uncle Drew, Little Mountain, and
enigmatic NBA superstar / Martin Gitlin.
Description: Lincoln: University of Nebraska Press, [2019]
| Includes bibliographical references and index.
Identifiers: LCCN 2019005775
ISBN 9781496213495 (cloth: alk. paper)
ISBN 9781496218445 (epub)
ISBN 9781496218452 (mobi)
ISBN 9781496218469 (pdf)
Subjects: LCSH: Irving, Kyrie, 1992– | Basketball players—
United States—Biography—Juvenile literature.
Classification: LCC GV884.I88 G57 2018 |
DDC 796.323092 [B]—dc23 LC record available at
https://lccn.loc.gov/2019005775

Set in Lyon by Mikala R. Kolander.
Designed by N. Putens.

I am dedicating this book to all the newspaper journalists who have maintained their dedication despite shrinking wages and circulation. All my friends in that world remain a source of inspiration to me.

Contents

Acknowledgments

I would like to acknowledge the following people for taking time out of their busy schedules to be interviewed for this book: Brady Klopfer, Bill Livingston, Rick Noland, Jeff Schudel, and Steve Wiseman. Thank you one and all!

Introduction

Some details are sketchy, others clear. It was a late-winter or early-spring afternoon in 2018. I was taking a break from my writing with a toasted cheese sandwich in one hand and TV remote in the other. Most certainly I was viewing a taped rerun of some show such as *The Twilight Zone* or *All in the Family* that my wife and kids cite as evidence of my perpetual childhood and refusal to link pop culturally into the twenty-first century.

This typical scene in my life was interrupted by an atypical phone call. I recognized the ID name immediately. It was Jeff Wechsler. Holy cow, I thought. That's the agent for Kyrie Irving. How he learned I was authoring a biography of his client was obvious to me before I answered. One of a few Irving associates I had contacted to interview for the book must have informed him. It's amazing how much speculation can filter through a mind in the moments it takes to pick up a phone.

Wechsler wasted no time getting to the point. He expressed unhappiness about the project. He was not impolite, but firm and far less than friendly. He did not want me writing the book, but he understood he could not stop me. He indicated he would urge those close to Irving to decline interviews. He made it clear that the extraordinarily gifted point guard would not speak with me. And before hanging up, he uttered seven words that will forever remain in my consciousness: "We control the narrative on Kyrie Irving."

That ship, of course, had sailed more than a decade earlier. What Wechsler either failed or refused to realize was that the media had controlled the narrative on Kyrie Irving from the moment his incredible talent began warranting such attention. Several years before the soon-to-be-superstar hired Wechsler as his agent and joined the Cleveland Cavaliers as the first overall pick in the 2011 draft, reports of his brilliance had surfaced. The narrative indeed had begun to be written and voiced.

But there would eventually prove to be far more to that narrative than his wizardry with a basketball. There was the emergence of an enigmatic young man both on and off the court. What followed were more questions than answers, all of which remained through the first seven years of his NBA career. Is Kyrie Irving a great player or merely a great talent? Is he motivated by team goals or only individual achievement? Does he raise the level of play of his teammates or even care to? Does he feel disdain for the media, using it only toward his own ends? And does this highly intelligent, well-spoken athlete really believe that the absurd claims of the Flat Earth Society are worthy of discussion?

One might argue that the paradox of Kyrie Irving negatively reflects modern thought. I have heard many in the sports media not only equate his outrageous offensive skills with all-around greatness despite his never having earned a spot on the first or second All-NBA team but also praise his flat-earth claim, questioning that the moon landing ever happened, and expressing wonderment over the existence of dinosaurs as bringing much-needed personality to the NBA—truth be damned.

I recall vividly a 1970 *Sports Illustrated* baseball article featuring maddeningly underachieving Cleveland Indians left-hander Sam McDowell, whom slugger Reggie Jackson believed to have boasted the finest fastball, curve, slider, and changeup he ever saw. Author Pat Jordan offered that, to McDowell, the ability to achieve a goal and achieving it are one and the same, as are owning the greatest talent and being the greatest pitcher.

Why then must he prove it? And in the end, McDowell proved nothing aside from demonstrating that talent alone sometimes triumphed.

The eventual revelation that alcoholism played a significant role in the demise of McDowell's career weakens any comparison to Irving. But it remains to be seen if Irving suffers a similar fate due to a seeming lack of desire to maximize his potential through equal attention to defensive efficiency and willingness to fully involve his teammates offensively, as well as what could be interpreted as a motivation to further his personal brand rather than grow into the best all-around player he can be.

Kyrie Irving is a fascinating, complex man whose inspirations cannot be easily identified. He has searched for happiness and contentment through personal reflection, music, acting, intellectual pursuits, and even a 2018 trip to a Sioux reservation. It was there he found his second family, that of his mother of Native American heritage, whom fate cruelly removed from his life at the age of four.

Most athletes are so intrinsically tied to their athletic pursuits and achievements that the media and international fandom identify them strictly with the sports they play. Irving, on the other hand, is quite the Renaissance man. He is Kyrie Irving, but he is also known as Uncle Drew and Little Mountain. Unlike many athletes who embrace the trappings of their fame and fortune, he seeks self-actualization through a variety of pursuits. His primary goal as a player is rising to challenges rather than earning "max" contracts. His dreams extend far beyond the NBA arena.

Yet he is the ultimate enigma. He is a learned intellectual who has expressed beliefs only accepted by the ignorant few. He speaks about his desire to win championships, yet demanded a trade away from the franchise best suited to deliver him a second one, and listed among his desired destinations were teams eons away from capturing a title. He speaks of maximizing his talent but works toward that end only on one side of the floor as a ball handler and finisher. He is in many ways a walking contradiction.

This biography will explore the mysteries of Kyrie Irving. There are many to unravel.

KYRIE IRVING

1 The Prodigy from Down Under

The toddler stared intently from the stroller. The intricacies of the action in front of him were beyond his comprehension, but he was too fascinated to look away. He gazed at men racing up and down the asphalt court. The thirteen-month-old watched all the basketball players, especially his dad, Drederick, who would occasionally saunter over with a bottle of milk to keep his son happy and fed.

It was the spring of 1993. The site was one of the legendary playgrounds of New York City, where pro-am league games entertained hoop-thirsty crowds. Not a soul showed greater interest than that young boy named Kyrie Irving, who yearned for a piece of the action after being freed from the constraints of his buggy. He invariably asked for a basketball and handled it remarkably well for his age, dribbling with one hand as his eyes remained fixed on his father. Proud papa kept footage of such scenes to prove to future doubters that his son could indeed handle the rock just a month beyond his first birthday.

The chip off the old block had a willing and loving role model. The man friends call Dred embraced the sport of basketball growing up alongside five siblings in the Mitchel Houses, a South Bronx project. He learned the value of industriousness and the struggles of solo parenting from his mother, Lillian, who was forced to raise her children alone after her husband abandoned the family when Drederick was six years old. She worked two jobs, took care of the kids, and still managed to further her education in community college.

Basketball proved an escape for the boy from the drugs, gangs, and guns that wreaked havoc with other neighborhood youths. Along with his best friend, Rod Strickland, who emerged as one of the premier point guards in a long and fruitful NBA career, Drederick honed his skills on the same courts to which he accompanied his son years later. He blossomed into a standout at Adlai E. Stevenson High School in the Bronx before landing a scholarship at Boston University, where he earned a degree in economics and shattered the school's all-time scoring record with 1,931 points as a six-foot-four shooting guard.

The elder Irving led the Terriers to four North Atlantic Conference title games and an NCAA Tournament berth in 1988. Ironically, they lost in the first round to Duke, where his son would nearly a quarter century later earn the spotlight as the finest college talent in the nation. Though Drederick remained undrafted, his potential proved intriguing enough to land him a tryout with the Celtics. His strengths and style of play did not meld with the Boston offensive system, but he tried to adapt to it rather than display his own skill set. After he failed to secure a roster spot, he was invited by fellow Boston University alum and future Philadelphia 76ers coach Brett Brown to join the Bulleen Boomers of the South East Australian Basketball League.

Drederick had by that time married the woman of his dreams. He had met Elizabeth Larson at a campus convenience store as a sophomore. Drederick recalled wistfully that his world stood still upon first glance despite her rather unsexy volleyball attire that included kneepads and red-and-white shorts. The couple struck up an immediate friendship before he began dating the woman he called "beautiful, inside and out."

The half-black, half-Native American freshman and adopted daughter of a Lutheran minister was a classically trained pianist and fine athlete who yearned to become president of the United States; she performed with an intensity on the court that reminded her father of Kyrie. "When Elizabeth played, she would get this look in her eye," said George Larson, her dad. "We called her Bessie Warbonnet. And her son plays basketball with the same look. You can see he zones everything out and he's just laser-focused."

Elizabeth Larson became Elizabeth Irving after Drederick's graduation and followed him to Melbourne, Australia. And on March 23, 1992, fourteen months after giving birth to daughter Asia, the couple welcomed into the world son Kyrie Andrew Irving, who was named by Elizabeth's minister father. Drederick's boyhood friend Strickland, who had already gained stardom with the San Antonio Spurs after a brief stint with his hometown Knicks, accepted a request to serve as Kyrie's godfather.

Drederick and Elizabeth had become quite the nomads before the birth of their son. They had moved cross-country to the Washington State town of Puyallup, where Asia was born, before relocating halfway around the world to Australia. Drederick destroyed the competition at that level, averaging 30 points per game for the Boomers, but their stay down under proved short-lived. They eventually returned stateside and settled near Seattle to raise the kids. Meanwhile, Drederick scoured Manhattan to seek work in the bond market. He sought the financial security for his family that he could never enjoy during his upbringing.

He would find it, but not before fate took a tragic turn. An overcast September day in early 1996 would prove far gloomier for the family when Elizabeth checked into Tacoma General Hospital with symptoms that would reveal a blood infection. Her condition headed downhill. Neither Drederick—nor his young children—could understand the depth of her plight. One can only imagine their monumental shock when she died at age twenty-nine from organ failure and an inflammatory condition known as sepsis syndrome. Four-year-old Kyrie was suddenly and shockingly motherless. No more would he fall asleep in her loving arms to the sweet strains of religious songs she learned from her father. All Kyrie would have to remember her by were stories from his dad and photographs.

Though Kyrie remembers little about his mother, he has faithfully and lovingly memorialized her. After gaining stardom in the NBA, he had her birth date, August 13, tattooed in roman numerals on the insides of his wrists, "VIII" on the left and "XIII" on the right. These same numerals are duplicated on the third edition of Kyrie's signature Nike sneakers. He also had a tattoo of her name with wings and a halo inscribed over his heart. "She's one of the reasons why I've come so far, why I have the drive that I do," he explained.

Those feelings remained with Kyrie to such an extent that he felt compelled in August 2018 to visit the Standing Rock Indian Reservation, home to the Sioux tribe into which Elizabeth had been born. He felt a sense of pride at a sacred naming ceremony in being given the Lakota name Hela, which translates to "Little Mountain." Irving spoke about the meaning of the experience to honor his mother while praising the inclusiveness of the Standing Rock Sioux Tribe and proclaiming them his second family.

Fortunately for the young Kyrie, his father, who was devastated at the loss of Elizabeth, refused to allow her death to diminish his parental duties. Quite the opposite—he became both a mother and father to his children. Only when his kids had been put to bed for the night did he feel free to cry himself to sleep. He strengthened his relationship with Kyrie as a friend, mentor, and teacher—even a character-building foe on the basketball court. Drederick also ensured their financial security by landing a job as a bond broker in Manhattan and settling the family in a fine neighborhood of West Orange, New Jersey.

The many roles of Drederick Irving often proved hectic and time-consuming. He demanded nothing from anybody. Rather than lament what many would consider overwhelming responsibilities, he embraced them with the help of his four sisters in the understanding that he was not alone. "A lot of women [are single parents] and they get no recognition," he said. "I don't want the recognition, to be honest with you. I just handled the responsibility as a father. There were challenges, but I think, overall, Kyrie and [Asia] have a good life, and I just tried to provide to the best of my abilities."

Basketball remained Drederick's passion, one that he sought to instill in his son. That was not a difficult task—the boy who could dribble one-handed soon after his first birthday not only associated the sport with his dad's love and attention but also simply enjoyed playing. As the younger Irving grew older, he learned more about his father's career. He came to understand the emotional and mental pain Drederick felt at failing to earn a spot in the NBA. That pain planted the seeds of Kyrie's desire to take his own budding talent to the ultimate level. He was inspired to track his height by scratching notches into his bedroom door and, in fourth grade, writing "I'm going to the NBA" and underlining "Promise" on a wall.

Drederick understood that such a goal would take far more than inspiration. Kyrie had the desire to maximize his talent at that age, but not the confidence on the court in the earliest stages of youth basketball. His father noticed that firsthand as the coach of his son's fifth-grade travel team. While his teammates reveled in displaying their natural abilities, Kyrie shied away. He watched the others while wandering around the court despite Drederick's appeals to show off his own gifts. The killer instinct that became a Kyrie trademark had yet to emerge, because it was not his natural state of mind.

"I worked on Wall Street for years, and I can tell you that Kyrie's not a type A personality," Drederick said. "Those people are really strong-minded. They don't lack in confidence. They try to dominate conversations. That wasn't Kyrie."

It wasn't only that. The young Kyrie, who years later would be criticized for hogging the ball and failing to involve his teammates offensively, felt compelled to please those that wore the same uniform rather than stuff his own stat line. But he also learned later in life that such a mind-set was the product of a lack of faith in his abilities. "I was afraid to be the best," he said. "Confidence, confidence, confidence: That's all my dad preached. He'd always tell me, *Kyrie, you could be this. You could be that.* My dad had more belief in me than I had in myself."

Drederick almost lost his chance to instill that confidence in his son when he had a narrow escape from the terrorist attacks of September 11,

2001. Drederick had spent several years working as a financial broker with Cantor Fitzgerald on the 105th floor of the World Trade Center. He then landed another job at Garvan Securities in the same building but, inexplicably, felt a sense of dread about it. Only those who believe in premonitions might claim that Drederick sensed disaster, but he did quit that job after only three weeks for one at Thomson Reuters on Financial Square.

Drederick walked through the World Trade Center building every morning from the train station, and the hustle and bustle of what seemed to be a typical scene was interrupted that fateful morning by a booming noise that sent him reeling. Bedlam ensued. Walls began to collapse as panicked people escaped the suffocating smoke and began to race for the exits, but stopped out of fear as debris descended from the sky. "I thought the boiler exploded," Drederick recalled. "The boom was so loud, the force of wind so powerful. There was shattered glass everywhere. . . . All I could think of was, 'I've got to get to my kids.' . . . I stuck my head out and tried to see, but I couldn't tell what it was. Pieces of the building, pieces of the plane, a lot of paper."

Drederick made a run for it, using the same elusiveness that came in handy on the basketball court, as he dodged hunks of steel falling from the building that would have added his name to the list of fatalities. He phoned his friends from Cantor Fitzgerald. No answer. He stared at the great skyscraper in flames and realized the horrifying, sickening truth. That was not debris coming off the World Trade Center. Those were bodies choosing forced suicide over burning up. It was an image that Drederick could not remove from his consciousness and gave him nightmares for years.

He knew how close to death he had been. Thoughts of his own demise raced through his mind. What if he hadn't escaped? What if he had been felled by a piece of metal hurtling down from a thousand feet? What would have happened to his children? Who would take care of them? As those frightening reminders of the fragility of life permeated his thoughts and emotions, he realized that the roads were blocked, trains were stilled, and phone lines were down. He began a nine-hour journey to return home.

Meanwhile, nine-year-old Kyrie felt the fears of uncertainty. He knew that his father no longer worked at Cantor Fitzgerald in the World Trade Center, but he was keenly aware that his daily routine passed him through the twin towers. He sat in school as harried parents arrived to escort other students away. His own comfort would have to wait as he experienced the tragedy of an unforgettable day. "There were a bunch of teachers crying, a bunch of them leaving the classroom," Kyrie said. "No one knew what was going on. Everyone left with their parents. My sister and I had to wait until school got out."

Even then, no father. They returned home to their babysitter and television reports of the horror that intensified the dread that Drederick was dead. He walked six hours and nine miles from Wall Street to the Bronx, where friend Larry Romaine drove him home to his relieved children in New Jersey.

The experience strengthened his resolve to play a significant role in the lives of Kyrie and Asia. He stressed education and athletics. He had enrolled them at a young age in a private school in New Jersey and yearned to provide Kyrie with the best hoops education he could find; so at weekends he accompanied him to the playgrounds near the Mitchel projects, where he had honed his skills as a youth. The games and the kids were tough there, and Dad wanted Kyrie to gain experience competing in what could be an unsettling on-court environment. The nine-year-old was at first intimidated by the trash-talking New Yorkers, motivating Drederick to give him a ninety-minute lecture on the fear of failure and the benefits of self-confidence against the most daunting competition. It was a pep talk that would inspire his son to greatness. He would later in life credit his father for the fierce competitive spirit he soon developed.

Drederick encouraged Kyrie to become well-rounded. The result for the boy who had inherited his mother's musical gifts was lessons in the trumpet, saxophone, and baritone horn. But Dad knew basketball best and was most successful teaching Kyrie the intricacies of that sport. He formulated a plan that would not only make the most of his physical skills but also cure him of any lingering fearfulness on the court through repetition. Father and son regularly played one-on-one games in their narrow driveway that encouraged Kyrie to attack the basket and take high-percentage shots.

Then there was the Mikan Drill, which was drilled into his head. Once Kyrie had completed his homework, Drederick would illuminate the driveway with his car lights and his son would shoot lay-ups. Right-handed. Left-handed. Right-handed. Left-handed. On and on and on into the night off a backboard missing part of its right side, forcing Kyrie to gain even greater accuracy. The smaller target aided him in learning to lay balls in with spin and finish despite difficult angles. Drederick would then appear with three cones, around which Kyrie practiced his ballhandling. He would dribble two balls simultaneously. He would dribble a tennis ball. He would dribble in-and-out, dribble at various speeds, dribble behind the back, and work on the crossover that would prove deadliest of all against exasperated NBA defenders. Kyrie learned to handle the basketball like it was a yo-yo and he was a yo-yo champion. Soon the competition in New Jersey and New York would be marveling at his amazing skills.

Among those duly impressed was future New Jersey governor Richard Codey, who often coached Irving in AAU games. Codey, whose son Chris later teamed with Irving at Montclair Kimberley Academy, recalled his impressions. "His instincts were tremendous," Codey said. "Like on a breakaway, he would slow up just enough to let the kid catch him and he could get the lay-up and the foul. And he did it better than any kid I've ever seen in my life."

Drederick knew his son was something special, but he wanted him to know it as well. "Like it or not," he told Kyrie, "God blessed you with a Bentley engine. If you don't go, the team doesn't go."

That Kyrie was blessed had become evident well before he reached high school. But to what extent he could use that enormous talent to maximize team success remained debatable nearly two decades later.

2 Rising Above the Ballers of Jersey

One could not have imagined when he was in eighth grade that Kyrie Irving would ever rise into the air and launch a jump shot to win an NBA championship, as he did over Golden State rival Steph Curry in 2016. After all, he was just five foot seven at the time and shot the ball from his hip as a member of the West Orange Traveling Team.

But the kid was certainly being coached up by his dad, who ran his players ragged for a reason. Drederick drilled his bunch like they were Duke Blue Devils preparing for the NCAA Tournament. They sometimes ran thirty laps around the gym before practice, then repeated intricate pick-and-roll schemes and backdoor plays. The undersized youths often felt overwhelmed, but Kyrie benefited greatly from the advanced lessons. He began showing glimpses of greatness.

Despite that potential, Drederick eschewed any motivation to enroll Kyrie in a basketball factory, opting instead for Montclair Kimberley Academy, a stately private school in New Jersey that produces far more Ivy League students than college athletes. The school's basketball coach Tony Jones had become aware of the young Irving when he first saw him play as an eighth grader during an AAU game in New Jersey. One play in particular motivated Jones to work with Drederick on luring the boy to the Cougars.

"The first thing I noticed more than anything, I'll never forget, he got the ball in transition, he was ahead of the pack, and this guy was racing to catch him, and he suddenly cut in front of the player and finished a really tough lay-up," Jones recalled. "As an eighth grader, he didn't circle and try to make a lay-up with his strong hand. He just cut, held the guy off and finished with a lay-up. I just said, 'Wow. That kid can play. He understands what's going on.' I worked hard to get him here. I thought he could change our program."

The smallish Irving fit right in with a Cougars basketball team that boasted no player taller than six foot one. But he immediately emerged as its premier talent. He averaged 16 points a game to earn County Freshman of the Year honors as his team hung around .500.

Irving had yet to develop the passion for basketball and desire to max-imize his potential while fulfilling the literal promise that he had made to himself and his father five years earlier. He had not set a mindful trajectory to the NBA. Though Jones believed him to be the best player he'd ever seen at the school, that was not saying much. Irving sometimes did not prepare for battle seriously. He even took a required swim test an hour before a game rather than reschedule it. Jones, however, was impressed that Irving never developed a mind-set of superiority despite boasting a level of talent far higher than that of his teammates.

"Not all the time do you get really, really good people who have an opportunity to achieve their dreams," Jones said. "Ky is so down-to-earth. Sometimes kids who have the kind of success he's had at his age have this kind of prima donna attitude. He has none of that. He's about as down-to-earth as you can be."

But despite his humbleness and immense talent, a troubling reality reared its ugly head at Montclair, one that would become more estab-lished in his three seasons with Cleveland preceding the return of LeBron James. That is, Irving failed to significantly improve his team. The Cou-gars finished 13-14 his freshman year and managed just a 14-8 record his sophomore season competing in the smallest-school division in the state. Exemplifying the disconnect between individual and team success was one game in which Irving scored 44 points, including 40 in the second half. The total was among the highest in the state that year, but Montclair still lost.

The level of talent separating Irving from the weak level of competition grew more evident in the 2008 Prep B playoffs in which he simply took over games. Included was the state finals against Collegiate, during which he fueled a 16–2 run to turn a close battle into a rout. Irving finished with 32 points, 14 rebounds, 5 assists, and 3 steals to delight his coach, who indicated that his players understood that their emerging star could lead them to a championship. "We're a small school," Jones said. "The kids understand what they have to do to win. Kyrie is a pretty special player and there's no jealousy."

Irving surpassed 1,000 points at Montclair and displayed an array of offensive wizardry far beyond what its fans had ever witnessed at that tier. His ballhandling, body control, and shotmaking with deft touch and heavy body English against taller defenders made his game appear to be that of a man among boys. He often lured opposing players by dribbling distant from his body, motivating them to swipe at the ball, then spinning away for a lay-up. Every one-on-one battle at Montclair proved a perpetual mismatch.

The teenager entertained and inspired others. Stories abound of Irving-related recollections from classmates. One claimed that Irving refused water or Gatorade during games, which convinced the storyteller that the kid was not mortal. Another remembered that Irving decided to try out for the football team as well and leaped high in the air to remarkably snag a pass, then left the field in the realization that he could get hurt playing that sport. Yet another recalled how unsuspecting crowds, unaware of his greatness, would be silenced five minutes into games after bearing witness to it.

That Irving had blossomed offensively was undeniable after a second year in which he averaged 27 points a game. Teammate Seth Bynum recalled how he had risen above the competition. "He was going to go by you if you got on top of him," Bynum said. "If you backed away, he was going to hit a three in your face."

Defenders within (and aside from) small high school opposition were learning the same as Irving piled up points, praise, and awards. He was ranked sixth among all New Jersey sophomores in August 2007 for his achievements with the Cougars and the AAU New Jersey Roadrunners. He exploded for 35 points the next month in the finals of the Fall Jam Fest. He was named Most Valuable Player of the Bill St. Bernard's Holiday Tournament in December by scoring 32 points in the title round.

Playing for a school with a class of about one hundred did not allow Irving to receive the recognition he had earned. He was only selected eighth-team all-state after leading Montclair Kimberley to the crown. He had scored 47 points in one game and 48 in another, motivating athletic director Todd Smith to nominate him for the "Faces in the Crowd" section of *Sports Illustrated*, but was rejected. It had become apparent he would need to fly the coop to receive deserved kudos. He had simply outgrown Montclair and its competition. Like the owner of a bird that had become too big for its cage, Jones understood that he needed to let the kid go. He called Drederick and offered his view that Kyrie could land a scholarship—perhaps at a college in the Patriot League such as Colgate or Holy Cross—if he transferred to a more prestigious basketball school. Drederick replied that he felt his son could earn a ride to an even bigger program. And he was right.

Dad also understood that Kyrie required grooming outside high school gymnasiums, so he elicited the help of local coach Sandy Pyonin, who claims to have mentored more than thirty future NBA players. Pyonin drilled Irving unconventionally in the boiling-hot, windowless basement court of the local Young Men's and Young Women's Hebrew Association, urging him to hop in various directions while dribbling and jack up offhanded sky hooks from the foul line. The fifty-something even played the young Irving one-on-one, one point at a time up to 100 points. Unusual as such methods were, they aided in the teenager's development. "He had unlimited energy," said Pyonin, who placed Irving on his team for a summer AAU event in Florida.

Irving grew quicker and stronger while shooting up three inches to five foot ten by the summer before his junior season. One man who noticed was Rae Miller, an assistant coach at powerful St. Patrick's, which had produced such NBA players as Samuel Dalembert and Al Harrington. His connection to Irving began barely a day after his wife had given birth to their first son. He sat "bored out of his gourd" in the hospital room when his best buddy called to inform him that Irving was playing nearby. Miller hightailed it out of there and watched Irving play one half with the Roadrunners. That was all he needed to see. The kid dominated on both sides of the ball, a whale in a sea of guppies. "He'd come down and pass the ball, the ball would bounce off the kid, he'd get it back and lay it in," Miller recalled a decade later. "He had to do everything."

St. Patrick's (renamed The Patrick School in 2012) was the polar opposite of Montclair Kimberley as a basketball factory. Montclair is a small private academy nestled in a staid suburban neighborhood. St. Patrick's sits in a tough urban area of Elizabeth. It opened in 1858 and remained the oldest Catholic parish high school in New Jersey. Its tiny gymnasium, splashed with green and gold, was used solely for practice—the team played its games at nearby Kean University against some of the biggest and premier foes from inside and outside the state. Irving would grow so enamored with the program that he'd donate a new gymnasium to The Patrick School in January 2018.

Drederick yearned to send his son there to add a sense of toughness to what was already remarkable ability. He understood that the physical play and significantly higher level of talent would challenge Kyrie in ways his former teammates and competition could not. But he showed up sans application, forcing the headmaster to reject Kyrie. And when archrival St. Anthony's (whose coach Bobby Hurley Sr. never responded to Drederick's request to enroll Kyrie there) signed several standouts from New York, it appeared that the St. Patrick's Fighting Celtics would be taking a back seat. That's when Miller decided he had to force the issue.

"I remember going back to our headmaster and saying, 'You know, if we want to compete next year, we need to make sure that Kyrie Irving can get into St. Pat's,'" Miller said. "I talked to our headmaster about this kid really wants to be at St. Pat's. He's a great kid, he's a heck of a student, and he's a hell of a player. After a while, he relented, and I had to patch up the broken fence with his dad just to get him to consider it."

Drederick believed he had Kyrie ready when his son walked through the doors of St. Patrick's. Dad knew he could play with the big boys because he saw it first-hand in consecutive games of one-on-one in which son blanked father 15–0. Not bad for a 16-year-old competing against a former major college standout. Not that Drederick was complaining. Most gratifying was that Kyrie displayed a killer instinct previously lacking. "I said, 'Ky, the way you beat me is the way you should beat a 42-year-old,'" Drederick recalled. "He killed me . . . it wasn't even a game. I felt good because he got me. He wasn't nice to me because I was his dad. . . . He destroyed me and was talking smack the whole game. To me it was validation that Kyrie was ready to move on to make that next step."

That next step was a doozy. Irving not only had to compete against far superior players, including future No. 2 overall NBA draft pick Michael Kidd-Gilchrist and North Carolina recruit Dexter Strickland, but he also had to prove himself to his new teammates as both tough and talented. What they perceived at first was a quiet, skinny kid with limited athleticism. What they eventually witnessed was the best player St. Patrick's had ever produced.

Such a development took time. Irving looked quite out of place when he arrived at his new school. Coach Kevin Boyle had picked soon-to-be teammate Chase Plummer to look after Irving and make certain the newcomer adapted well to his unfamiliar surroundings. When Plummer first spotted Irving in the hallway, the newcomer was wearing his school uniform untucked with a mismatched vest. Plummer could hardly believe his eyes.

Neither could his fellow players when they first laid eyes on Irving. He didn't exactly look like the second coming of Michael Jordan. "He didn't have facial hair, had a big head—he just looked like a squirrel," said teammate Christopher Gibson. "We called him Squirrel Boy."

Soon the players donned their gray shorts and green T-shirts and chose sides for a pickup game. Irving played shyly at first, then suddenly escaped a trap by firing the ball through the legs of a defender, recaptured control of it, pulled it back to create space, and shot. Gibson quickly changed his tune. "It was amazing," he said. "He was doing stuff we'd never seen before." Added fellow teammate Kevin Seabrook, "He was ahead of everyone mentally."

But Irving was just months removed from dominating at Montclair Kimberley. Despite his flashes in practice, the transformation proved far from immediate. The overwhelming change in environment and significant upgrade in competition prevented him from transferring that killer instinct he displayed against Drederick to the courts on which St. Patrick's competed. It was a chicken-and-egg conundrum. He could not feel compelled to place the spotlight on himself until he earned the respect of his teammates and Fighting Celtics coach Boyle, who had never seen him play before his arrival. But his teammates would not believe in him until he showed off a bit.

"On a team with no other stars, he was the big fish in a small pond," said Miller in reference to Montclair Kimberley. "Come into this pond, and there's sharks in there, and he wasn't sure if he was a goldfish or a shark. It took some time for him to be comfortable being a shark. . . . His dad wanted to know how he would fit in. Coach Boyle told him, 'I won't promise you ever that he'll start or play, but if he doesn't start or play he needs to look in the mirror.' We knew how good he was."

Soon everybody did. Irving toiled tirelessly. The kid who once scheduled a swim test an hour before a game emerged as a gym rat, hoisting up shots hours after his teammates had headed home. Miller eventually believed Irving was ready to be seen by major college coaches. The result was the sudden appearance of Duke legend Mike Krzyzewski to a practice. An overwhelmed Irving performed horribly, shooting bricks and looking uncomfortable. Worried that "Coach K" would permanently lose interest,

Miller put in a good word for Irving. Krzyzewski confirmed that he knew all about Irving's talent already. He even uttered words that were music to Irving's ears: "You'll be one of the best of your generation."

That prediction appeared quite bold given his uneven performance as a junior. He was sidelined the first thirty days of the season due to his transfer, then spent much of his on-court time after his return in mid-January hanging around the perimeter and passing the ball. Coaches sometimes felt compelled to order him to run plays for himself at the end of games.

Not that Irving didn't show glimpses of brilliance. In a shocking blowout of powerful St. Benedict's in early February 2009, he scored 21 points. That inspired Boyle to proclaim Irving as one of the greatest high school guards to ever play in New Jersey and perhaps the premier junior in the country. Boyle received criticism for what seemed at the time to be far-fetched declarations, but they'd prove to be prophetic.

Irving compiled impressive numbers as a junior, averaging 17 points, 6 assists and 2 steals per game. But his quiet and unaggressive nature on the court concerned teammates and coaches alike. He admitted later in life that he rarely talked to others. He remained in his shell throughout a season that ended in a third state title in four years for St. Patrick's.

The shell was left behind that spring and summer. Irving emerged as the finest prep point guard in the nation. The graduation of Dexter Strickland placed him front and center at that position on the Fighting Celtics. Irving understood that the team required his talent and experience as the quarterback of the offense and he fulfilled that necessity, playing with a level of swagger and confidence previously unseen during the off-season. He became a leader and a force as a scorer, winning Most Valuable Player honors at the Nike Global Challenge by averaging 21.3 points a game to lead the USA East to the tournament title.

In the summer of 2009, he flew to Orlando with his St. Patrick's teammates for the annual Super Showcase event. He was forced into a starring role sans Kidd-Gilchrist, who had opted to play with his AAU team. Irving scored 59 points in two games to key upsets of opponents led respectively by Kidd-Gilchrist and future Ohio State standout and NBA forward

Jared Sullinger. Between games, Irving hung out with his friends from the Roadrunners and distributed cups of water. He was blossoming as a player and as a person. "Everything changed for Kyrie that day," offered Duke assistant coach Chris Collins. "It was the day he figured out how good he was."

Irving was also growing mentally and emotionally. In a survey taken for USA Basketball, he listed fellow hoops standout Harrison Barnes as the most impressive person he had met, because of his intellectual maturity, and mentioned reading and writing as hobbies he enjoyed off the court. Irving became more outgoing and assertive, spreading his wings after returning to school for his senior year while exploring his acting and musical interests.

The senior embraced an opportunity to take a small but significant role in a production of *High School Musical* that included a short solo. Though other basketball players participated in the play, one of them offered that Irving was more into it than any of them. "One time he knew I wasn't singing the lyrics," recalled Kevin Seabrook. "Kyrie would look at me and make sure the teacher would see it, so I had to sing the part in front of everyone by myself." Though Irving missed his cue on the first night of two performances, the approximately one hundred patrons were surprised at his fine voice when he finally belted out a loose interpretation of his verse.

Irving, however, did not enroll at St. Patrick's to blossom into an *American Idol* winner. His goal was to compete against the best basketball teams. And when they identified Irving and his team on their schedules, that brought out the best in them. It was exactly what Irving needed to maximize his own effectiveness. "Every night we were going to play somebody that wanted to kill us," he recalled. "We had to be tough all the time. Everyone was coming after us." And that's exactly what Drederick had in mind when he enrolled his son at a basketball factory. "When he transferred to St. Patrick's, and he was subjected to playing against the best in the state of New Jersey, not to mention the top programs in the country, and I saw him dominate against those kids, that's when it registered that he was special," said the elder Irving.

Such lofty predictions remained unfulfilled until the summer before his senior season. And when his final year at St. Patrick's rolled around, Irving was ready. He had become fanatical about his workouts, which included morning and afternoon sessions with his team, and another well into the evening. Weekends were not spent hanging out with friends—Irving remained comparatively unsocial—but rather adding to his already impressive offensive repertoire by sending shots at various angles through the basket at home alongside his father.

The work paid off, but not before Irving and his teammates received bad news as they awaited a showdown at home against national power Oak Hill Academy. The deliverer of the verbal punch in the gut was an assistant coach, who announced that St. Patrick's had been banned from the New Jersey Tournament of Champions, which crowned the state titlist, due to a preseason workout rule violation. The school had appealed the punishment to no avail. Irving broke into tears. Kidd-Gilchrist tried to console him without success. But Irving refused to allow the disappointment to affect his performance. Both he and the future Charlotte Bobcats standout scored 28 points that night against the Oak Hill Warriors.

But in that battle Irving learned a lesson that Drederick hoped would last a lifetime. The man once nicknamed Iceman by his Boston University teammates for his ability to stay cool in the heat of battle chastised his son, who had passed the ball to teammate Derrick Gordon with the game on the line. Gordon missed two foul shots to turn a potential victory into a defeat. "Hey, did you guys see Kyrie play tonight?" Drederick asked Kyrie's friends. "I didn't see him out there. Did anyone else see him?" The point had been made. Father wanted son to take over in critical moments. The young man who had blossomed into the best finisher among prep players throughout the country needed to finish when it mattered most.

Whether the young Irving embraced that attitude from that point forward can be debated. But he would certainly perform with that mind-set in the NBA—just ask Steph Curry.

Irving became a hot commodity. He averaged 24.5 points and 6.5 assists per game his senior season. Coaches from premier college programs throughout the country expressed interest. But when Krzyzewski sent a handwritten note to the Irving home in West Orange, the die was cast. Though Kentucky (which at the time employed his godfather Rod Strickland in an administrative role) and Texas A&M were considered finalists for his services, Irving yearned to wear the uniform of the Duke Blue Devils, who had ended his father's Boston University career in the first round of the 1988 NCAA Tournament.

Kyrie Irving was about to reach a new level in his meteoric rise. But it would prove to be a short stop on route to his ultimate destination.

3 Steppingstone to Stardom

Kyrie Irving has understood the importance of self-motivation from childhood. His "promise" to himself in fourth grade created a physical, mental, and emotional pathway to the NBA, periodically confirmed by entries in a personal journal that reminded him of the inspiration required to achieve his goals. Upon his arrival at St. Patrick's, he wrote the following: *The lights are on, baby. Time to show the world what you're really about and who the best is in the country.* And six months later, when AAU competition separated the best from the rest, he added this: *I'm going to make it, even if I have to run through a ton of walls . . . F— being friends. I'm going to destroy these dudes.*

Irving did not always perform on the court with the same level of self-assurance indicated in such declarations, particularly early in his career with the Fighting Celtics. But his vision for the future and the intensity with which he pursued his dreams proved undeniable. That certainly remained the case after he continued his journey with the USA Basketball Men's U-18 National Team. So impressive was his tryout that he was told within four minutes that he had made the team, which he led to the FIBA Americas gold medal the summer before he arrived on the Duke campus to play for legendary coach Mike Krzyzewski. The undefeated Americans eked by Brazil to clinch the championship behind Irving, who led the team with 21 points, 10 rebounds and 5 assists.

By that time Irving had shed all insecurities about his basketball talent. He transformed preseason pickup games into personal displays of offensive wizardry and isolation dominance. Irving showed moves on the court that his teammates, as well as past Blue Devils such as former point guard and 2002 overall second NBA pick Jay Williams, had never witnessed. Williams, for one, soon realized that Irving would be one-and-done at Duke. Nothing that Irving would do on the court that year would dissuade anyone that he wouldn't take his talents to the next level after one season with the Blue Devils. Nothing, that is, except a freak right-toe injury that threatened to derail what seemed to be a ride of destiny to the NBA.

Irving's skills were tested three months before the freshman donned a Duke uniform. He competed in a pro-am summer league in Durham in which he made his debut in what is known as The Triangle, the area encompassing North Carolina State, North Carolina and Duke. He showed flashes of the brilliance that would eventually catapult him atop the list of college prospects. Irving had watched highlights of future Washington Wizards standout point guard John Wall as he dominated pro-am league play in North Carolina and sought to follow in Wall's sneaker steps. Irving scored 35 points in his first game against a team led by Kansas State standout Dominique Sutton. He understood that the defensive challenges would prove beneficial against premier Atlantic Coast Conference and inevitable NCAA Tournament competition. "There are a lot of great players out here," Irving exclaimed. "You saw [Sutton] pick me up full court, and I need that. Especially in the league that I'm playing in this year."

Not even the nervousness associated with a major college debut and the pressure of starting as a freshman for arguably the most storied college basketball program in the nation at age 18 prevented Irving from dominating from the beginning. Krzyzewski bestowed upon him the honor of wearing the cherished No. 1 jersey and he lived up to it in his Duke debut despite the inevitable nervousness he later admitted to feeling. As would prove to be a pattern upon his arrival in a new environment—including years later in his first weeks with the Boston Celtics—he performed equally hard on the defensive end against overwhelmed Princeton. Irving blocked a shot and stole a crosscourt bounce pass in the first two Tiger possessions. He scored 17, shot 50 percent from three-point range, and dished out 9 assists.

Princeton senior guard Dan Mavraides was duly impressed. "Kyrie's natural talent, in-game awareness, knack for the basketball—that's a rarity, right?" he said. "You see the spins he puts on the ball, the way he finishes around traffic. It's obviously something he's worked on his whole life. It's damn near an innate ability."

The theme remained the same in opponent and teammate interviews until the toe injury that nearly wiped out the rest of his season. One and all were awe-struck at the on-court and off-court maturity of the mere freshman. They marveled at his court vision. Miami of Ohio junior forward Julian Mavunga could hardly believe what he witnessed after an easy Duke victory over his team. "That kid, at 18, was getting guys in the huddle," he recalled. "He was coming down the court, and he wasn't looking at [Krzyzewski] on the sideline. He was . . . calling plays. He'd see mismatches and be like, 'Okay we gotta get this guy the ball.' He has this sense for the game—not only to score, not only to pass, or be the creator, but to just help other people on the basketball court."

The praise just kept on coming. But, as Duke continued to roll over the comparative weak sisters of college basketball, Irving had yet to experience a challenging level of competition. He received greater defensive attention and pressure against the likes of Marquette and Michigan State. Most impressive was his performance against the rugged Michigan State Spartans, who featured future Golden State Warriors star and annual NBA Finals nemesis Draymond Green. Green claimed later that he knew little about Irving before their first battle, but he certainly gained knowledge the hard way. Irving threw his personal kitchen sink at the Big Ten power with offensive weaponry that resulted in 31 points on 8-of-12 shooting. Most impressive was his ballhandling that allowed him to tally in traffic and force fouls of frustration. Irving took up residence at the line, nailing 13 of 16.

Among those covering the action at raucous Cameron Indoor Stadium was Duke beat writer and eventual *Durham Herald-Sun* sports editor Stephen Wiseman. He had long before lost any feeling of surprise at Irving's bag of tricks. But that performance against Michigan State was a coming-out party of sorts, because Irving had previously averaged only 14 points and taken 9 shots per game. He proved far more aggressive in a contest that received national attention against the finest foe Duke had played to date.

"We did wonder how he would adjust to being a freshman starting point guard for a team that had just won a national championship," Wiseman recalled. "I thought he was a good scorer, not a great shooter—though he could shoot a little bit—but his ability to find lanes to the basket and score in traffic, put the ball off the backboard, and score that way really stood out. I remember that game against Michigan State and just thinking, 'Wow, this might be one of the best college players in the country.'"

One of the best college players in the country nearly didn't play another full college game. Three nights later, in a rematch of the 2010 national championship against tough Butler, which was ironically led by his future Celtics coach Brad Stevens, Irving had recovered from a 4-point, zero-assist first half that motivated Krzyzewski to criticize him at halftime for his inaction to score 17 quick points. But disaster struck late in the second half when Irving drove the baseline, pulled up, and slammed his toe against the foot of Butler forward Matt Howard. It didn't seem like much at the time, but Irving did limp off the court. He soon returned, however, and played another two minutes.

Little did he realize that he had torn ligaments in his right toe. He woke up the next morning in enough pain to require further examination that revealed the damage that ruled him out indefinitely. He later revealed that he had been born with an extra sesamoid bone in his right toe, which resulted in the torn connective ligaments. The severity and uniqueness of the injury motivated Duke medical personnel to send Irving to renowned foot surgeon Dr. Bob Anderson. Irving eventually decided to rehab the toe rather than undergo a surgery that would have guaranteed his absence for the remainder of the season. Krzyzewski was not sure that such a plan of attack would prove wise. He figured Irving would not make it back that season.

Irving toiled endlessly to prove him wrong. While his teammates practiced he spent two hours a day in rehab. He worked to strengthen his toe in the pool and eventually took on weight-bearing exercises. He was sometimes in a cast and otherwise in a walking boot or using a carbon-fiber shank in his shoe to decrease stress on the toe. Irving hated the process and lamented the emotional and mental damage as much as the physical challenges.

"I'm not going to sugarcoat it," Irving said. "It has been really tough, just seeing my teammates getting ready for games in the lay-up line and just the ball being tipped. I miss that feeling being out in Cameron and playing away games and big-time games on ESPN. I miss all those moments because those were opportunities that I wanted to see, especially during my freshman year, and all that being taken away from you it's hard to really understand, and you always question why did this happen to me? But I think I have grown. I've grown mentally and physically throughout this whole process. I have kept my faith and I think that is what's getting me through this."

The support Irving received proved inspirational. Though he credited his father and sister Asia with buoying his spirits, he also praised his fellow Duke students, some of whom launched a website they creatively called savekyriestoe.com. Irving did not lose touch with his teammates, either, joking with them during workouts and partaking in the choreographed personalized handshakes that had become all the rage on basketball courts. His fellow players reveled in what they believed to be their obligation to ensure his positive mind-set. It was an effort Irving greatly appreciated.

That was not all Irving appreciated during his recovery. He also grew from the intellectual stimulation and education he was receiving at a prestigious institution, one that demanded of him the attention to class-work many other schools did not ask of their premier athletes. Irving considered returning to Duke for his sophomore year, not only because the toe injury threatened to end his freshman season quite prematurely and perhaps before he could experience March Madness but also because he valued the opportunity to expand his mind. Basketball remained his primary focus; he was driven to greatness on the court. But nobody could accuse Irving of being a one-dimensional person. Wiseman believes his exploration of other interests in college played a role in his consideration of sticking around another year.

"I thought the kid probably likes going to Duke," Wiseman said. "He likes going to class, so much so that after he got hurt and came back there was a little bit of doubt about whether he would go to the NBA in some of our minds because he seemed to like going to school and liked the learning aspect of being at Duke. That's why it blew me away when this whole flat-earth thing came about. I didn't see that coming at all because he's a pretty smart kid. He does have that side to him that basketball isn't everything."

Irving was also developing a side unappreciated by the media that would worsen after his arrival in the NBA. Sports reporters struggled to identify the issue. It seemed to be neither aloofness nor arrogance, but rather a dismissive attitude toward reporters. The lack of enthusiasm for interviews that did not further his brand or prove beneficial to him personally was evident during his one year at Duke and became more pronounced thereafter.

"I wouldn't describe him as being an open book by any stretch of the imagination," said Wiseman, who theorized that the eighteen-year-old Irving had yet to fully emerge from his shell. "I remember having one sit-down, one-on-one interview with him that was for a deep-drive kind of story that we couldn't run because he got hurt and the story took a different turn. I wouldn't describe it as an awful experience—you just had to push him to open up. He was pretty good in postgame settings, but nothing special. It wasn't a situation where you felt, god, I have to talk to Kyrie and it's going to be a pain. Maybe it was all because he was just young and finding his way. It was his first time in a major media setting. Duke is pretty high profile."

Irving missed the entire conference schedule as the Blue Devils blitzed the competition, winning their first fifteen games, finishing the regular season with a 27-4 record, then steamrolling through the ACC Tournament, winning all three contests by at least 14 points. He got the smallest taste of that event, warming up with his teammates before the final's dismantling of sixth-ranked North Carolina that served as a prelude to the NCAA Tournament for the top-seeded Blue Devils. As his team prepared for an inevitable pounding of hapless Hampton in the first round, Irving spoke about the possibility of participating. Krzyzewski finally announced that his freshman point guard would emerge from the bench and play limited minutes.

That proclamation changed everything. It not only seemingly maximized Duke's potential to win a second consecutive national title, but it helped punch a ticket for Irving to the professional ranks. "I truly believe that I wouldn't have come out [for the NBA draft] if I only played eight games," Irving said later that year. "Number one, I came back to prove to everyone that I was ready [for the NBA]. And number two, I wanted to stop all the questions whether I was healthy enough, whether this toe injury would have a lingering effect on my career. If I didn't play in the NCAA tournament, I wouldn't have come out."

Critics of Irving might have cited what they would consider a telling omission. What he did not include as an inspiration was the opportunity to help his team earn another crown. That leaves the impression of Irving as a young man motivated more by individual goals than contributing to group achievements and sharing the elation with teammates that comes with winning championships. Such a perception reared its ugly head again years later when he demanded a trade from a Cleveland team that had made annual trips to the NBA Finals and was reportedly listed among his preferred destinations with the downtrodden New York Knicks and also-rans Miami and Minnesota.

Others might claim such criticism unwarranted. Irving certainly talked a good game upon his return for March Madness, stating that it was a bond with his Duke teammates and loyalty to Krzyzewski that led to a desire to return for his sophomore season. That he toiled so diligently to overcome the toe injury and make himself available for the NCAA Tournament could be interpreted as a way to prove to the NBA he was ready, but it could also be perceived as a desire to help the Blue Devils claim another crown.

Whatever the perception, Irving required more time to return to his pre-injury greatness. Krzyzewski estimated his effectiveness at about 50 percent when Duke began its quest for a title against overwhelmed Hampton. Irving played just twenty minutes in a game that was over around tip-off and he scored 14 points with just 1 assist. He did show flashes, such as an isolation play in which he torched his defender with a wicked crossover and buried a three-pointer two feet beyond the line. "I'm back! I'm back!" Irving proclaimed as he pounded on his chest.

Not really. He was still shaking off the rust in his second game in forty-eight hours when the Blue Devils battled Michigan in Charlotte for a spot in the Sweet Sixteen. He nailed just one shot but attacked the basket effectively enough to visit the foul line ten times. Yet Krzyzewski trusted him to put the ball in his hands in the final minute to protect a 70–69 lead. Irving rose to the occasion, scoring his only hoop of the game on a banker as his team held on for dear life.

The legend of Kyrie was growing. Michigan guard Josh Bartelstein felt it. "It was basically a home game for Duke . . . and you could feel it," he said. "Every time he'd dribble in warm-ups or run on the court, it was kind of like a mythical experience. Like this guy is actually playing . . . he's healthy. You had a sense there was something bigger going on. It's hard to quantify . . . but people were so fascinated by the player he was going to be."

The player he was going to be became a bit more apparent when Duke battled Arizona four days later. Irving proved himself ready for the NBA despite a defeat that ended his college career. Irving performed more assertively, attacking the basket and befuddling defenders in scoring 28 points off the bench. He took 15 shots—three more than he had in the first two games of the tournament combined. He simply could not match the performance of Wildcats forward Derrick Williams, who bullied his way into the conversation about who would be selected first in the NBA draft with 32 points and 13 rebounds.

Irving claimed after the game that he preferred to return to Duke for his sophomore season. He was left feeling empty. "I'll never forget that game," he said years later. "I felt like there was more than I wanted to get out of playing with Coach K, playing with great players on a college level. I was just so excited about the opportunity to go after something bigger than ourselves . . . I was definitely considering staying. There was a strong feeling. . . . I wanted to stay, truth be told."

He might have indeed stuck around if not for the insistence of his father and Krzyzewski that he declare for the draft. They believed he had proven all he could at the college level despite having played in only eleven games. After all, he was the likely No. 1 pick. There was nowhere else to go but down. And he had already sustained a significant injury. In retrospect, what if the knee injury that would force him to miss the 2015 NBA Finals and much of the 2017–18 season, including all of the playoffs, had been sustained in an imaginary sophomore year at Duke? He could not take that chance. And, indeed, Irving announced on April 6, 2011, that he was turning pro. The Cleveland Cavaliers were licking their chops. Debates raged over whether they should take Williams or Irving. But there was little doubt in their minds that they needed to land the isolation assassin.

4 Rocking and Rolling to Cleveland

History frowned upon Kyrie Irving after he declared himself eligible for the 2011 NBA draft. The league had been particularly brutal to young point guards, a position that requires complete court awareness that only comes with experience. During its open-door policy to players fresh out of high school, the NBA had welcomed only three point guards from the prep ranks. The immensely talented Sebastian Telfair never panned out, Shaun Livingston grew into a solid bench contributor, and it took Lou Williams a decade to reach his potential as a super sixth man. One could understand the skepticism surrounding Irving as the draft approached. The always-opinionated Hall of Famer and basketball analyst Charles Barkley expressed what other critics believed when he stated, "He's not going to be no immediate help to my team."

That Barkley cited University of Kentucky point guard and eventual Pistons draftee Brandon Knight as a better prospect helps prove the impossibility of consistently predicting success. The Cavaliers, who owned the first selection, never considered Knight, who forged a fine career but through his first seven seasons did not reach the level of Irving or fellow point guard Kemba Walker. The other possibility for Cleveland was Derrick Williams, but he was a man without a set position. He was a classic "tweener" who did not fit ideally into the small-forward or power-forward mold. "As good as Derrick Williams played, I think everybody who had been around Kyrie kind of figured he was going to be the number one pick," said Duke forward Mason Plumlee.

Irving forged a unique and refreshing approach to turning professional. He signed with agent Jeff Wechsler, who represented only three other NBA players. They met shortly after the NCAA Tournament and included the chairman of a publicly traded company who offered the soon-to-be-wealthy Irving the sound advice of saving half the earnings from every paycheck. The founder of the nonprofit group Best Buddies, which nurtures friendships and employment opportunities for those with intellectual and developmental disabilities, sought to engage Irving as a way for him to remain grounded and help the less fortunate. Irving, who moved in with Wechsler's family in South Florida, heeded all the advice. He began volunteering at Best Buddies in Miami and set up an account he called Kyrie's Bucket that would allow him to undertake charitable endeavors.

He also worked out with the Cavaliers before the draft. They owned not only the first pick, but the fourth as well, which they used to snag University of Texas power forward/center Tristan Thompson. The setup allowed them to fill two holes at once. Irving expressed excitement over the possibility of being selected by Cleveland. "It's a rebuilding team," he acknowledged. "Whoever goes there, the pressure is going to come regardless. Just being in the top three [picks] has pressure. It will be a lot harder in Cleveland knowing that LeBron [James] left. But whoever is picked there should just worry about themselves and being focused on bringing a new culture to the team and contributing as much as they can."

Cavaliers vice president of basketball operations David Griffin, who eventually shaped his team into a world champion before a falling out with owner Dan Gilbert sent him packing, assumed the same. They soon made it official, though Derrick Williams was not informed he would be going second to Minnesota until less than two minutes before the announcement on draft night.

The dream of a fourth grader had become a reality. Irving had fulfilled the promise he had written on the wall of his home closet at age ten to reach the NBA. But the league was not reaching back—at least not that summer. A lockout that would wipe out the first two months of the regular season shifted his focus from basketball to continuing his education. He rented a house off-campus in Durham and, majoring in psychology, took four classes after promising his father that he would earn his degree within five years. He worked out occasionally with his former Duke teammates but played little basketball in the off-season. The Cavaliers were only allowed to have contact with him for one week between the June draft and July 1, during which time it was suggested he remain idle to allow his toe to fully heal. Such a request was not easily fulfilled for a gym and playground rat, especially since he declared himself healthy.

"It was the hardest two months of my life," Irving said. "It was hard to sit on the sidelines. Especially with the amount of exposure everyone was getting in playing in those pro-ams and being everywhere. That was different for me, not being able to work out and get better. Summertime is when my game has gone to a different level every year and that's happened throughout my entire life. It was a learning experience."

Irving anticipated sharing the point guard spot with incumbent starter Baron Davis, whom he claimed to have idolized since childhood. But Davis was not long for Cleveland. The man who Irving looked forward to mentoring him was waived by the Cavaliers two weeks before the regular season began, deemed unneeded with a wunderkind in the fold.

Though the nineteen-year-old rookie had indeed taken it easy that summer, Irving showed little sign of rust when training camp finally opened. He understood the expectations of title-starved fans, teammates, and the organization. One and all were just a year removed from "The Decision," a regrettable spectacle played in front of a national television audience in which Akron's own LeBron James, who had failed through little fault of his own to lead a Cleveland team to its first major sports championship since 1964, announced he was "taking his talents to South Beach" and the Miami Heat. They were also one year removed from a twenty-six-game losing streak, which at the time was the longest in NBA history; and one year removed from the letter written in anger by owner Dan Gilbert that called LeBron out for his "cowardly betrayal." The Cavaliers and their fans considered the drafting of Irving as the first major step in the recovery process.

So curious was the entire organization that they packed the practice facility in the centrally located suburb of Independence to watch Irving scrimmage against veteran Cleveland point guards Ramon Sessions and Jannero Pargo. Rather than dangle his feet in the water, feeling out his opponents and seeking a way to fit in, Irving embraced attack mode verbally and physically. "He was killing them," said power forward Samardo Samuels. "Talking shit . . . incredible finish after incredible finish."

The self-assurance and promise of newly acquired wealth delivered via a rookie contract exceeding $5 million a year did not translate into an embracing of the lifestyle of the rich and famous. Irving remained decidedly down-to-earth. Before the draft he lived with Wechsler while working out twice a day with a trainer at the University of Miami. He joked to the media that among the purchases with his first NBA check would be a pair of dress socks. He returned to New Jersey after the draft to be with his beloved father, who spoke about the dream that had come true and the magnitude of what his son had accomplished.

That Irving boasted the talent to justify his selection atop the NBA draft proved undeniable from the start. But questions required answers. Many of them revolved around motivation. Would he be driven to fulfill his potential as an all-around player or simply as a scorer? Would he work as hard on the defensive end as he did on offense? Would he prioritize as a point guard the involvement of his teammates? Would he work to maximize potential win totals of a team woefully lacking in talent or seek only to establish his own offensive greatness?

The answers would not be fully revealed in a day, a week, even a month. But immediate impressions proved to be lasting ones. Irving drew gasps of amazement from those who witnessed the crossover, the jukes, the impossible angles, and the sweet kisses with English off the backboard that dropped through the net. But he played defense with little intensity and looked for his shot first, second, and third before seeking out open teammates. Among those who soaked it all in was veteran Cavaliers beat reporter Rick Noland of the *Medina Gazette*. He understood the limitations of the team in the early post-LeBron era. But he believed Irving could have done far more individually to further the Cavaliers' development.

"I think he's an AAU product and he grew up in that environment and played that type of game," Noland said. "Great moves are what draw the raves and reviews and that can be to the detriment of the easy, simple basketball play. I'm not saying Kyrie wasn't a smart player, but he didn't always do the easiest things before he looked for his own shot.

"He had to carry such a big load on the offensive end, and any player has to learn how to take mini-breaks on the floor to play that many minutes. But he rarely gave maximum effort on [defense]. And he has the physical tools. You can't be that good of an offensive player and that quick and have that ability to get to the basket and not have the tools to be a good defender, which he was for small stretches. It was more want-to. He was pretty doggone bad. When it came to fighting through picks, when a high screen is being set on you, you can with some effort and want-to a lot of times wedge your way through the top of that screen. He almost never did that. He would let his man go first and trail around it, which in turn made the big man help and by then the offense has already created the mismatch it's looking for.

"He talked a good game. Games they did win, he'd say, 'It's all about our defense, we have to play good defense, when we play defense we get out on the open court and we run.' That's because he's a really smart guy, really good when the cameras go on. He knows what the fans what to hear, knows what the coach wants to hear. But that doesn't mean he does it on the court too often with a high degree of intensity and effort."

Not that the Cavaliers expected Irving to right the ship by himself. Team vice president Griffin, who later criticized the poor culture of accountability within the organization at the time, believed Irving to be directionless as a rookie, and beyond, before James returned. The team was busy dumping assets and acquiring cap space to build for the future. Griffin believed that Irving, rather than trying to figure out what the Cavaliers sought to achieve on any given night, opted instead to flash and own talent and improve his skills at the highest level of basketball.

That does not explain, however, why Irving did not work to advance his abilities in all aspects of the game, including defense and passing. That he is an off guard forever trapped in a point guard's body is undeniable. But the growing number of critics throughout his career offer that such an anomaly is no excuse for keeping wide-open teammates waiting with hands waving in the air and leaving opponents open to drive right past him. That is not what he claimed to have had in mind when he scribbled down his goals for his rookie season that included "lead the team in defense."

Cavaliers coach Byron Scott certainly knew he had fallen woefully short in that pronouncement. "I always tell Kyrie, 'We know what you can do on the offensive end,'" said Scott, whose team ranked near the bottom of the NBA in defensive efficiency before and after Irving arrived. "But if you want to be an All-Star? If you want to be a complete basketball player and not a one-hit wonder, you gotta defend. You gotta do the little things."

Big things, little things. It didn't matter. Irving was terrible in all defensive tasks as a rookie. He ranked 447th among NBA players in allowing 1.03 points per possession. He struggled in all situations, including isolation, pick-and-roll, and spot-up defense. And the team played far better on that end of the floor with him not on it. The Cavaliers surrendered 107.6 points per forty-eight minutes with Irving on the bench. That number rose to 112.6 with him in the game.

Irving did at least attempt the big things with games on the line—successfully or unsuccessfully. He was consistently called upon by Scott to attempt game-winning shots. It took James nearly three seasons to sink one, but it took Irving a mere nineteen games. He beat host Boston by twirling through traffic for a left-handed lay-up as his father watched from the stands. He doomed Dallas by sliding past three defenders and scoring from the other side. He nailed two at the line to bury Sacramento. He downed Denver with a right-handed banker from the left side of the rim. So confident was Irving in his isolation invincibility that, during Team USA camp in July, he challenged his hoops hero Kobe Bryant to a one-on-one battle for fifty grand.

By that time, he had concluded a rookie season in which he led the team with averages of 18.5 points and 5.4 assists per game. He had shot a solid 47 percent from the floor and 40 percent from three-point range. The Rookie of the Year balloting provided as much surprise as a January snowfall in Cleveland. He received 117 of 120 first-place votes from a nationwide panel of writers and broadcasters—only the three that selected either Kawhi Leonard or future Cavaliers teammate Iman Shumpert prevented Irving from becoming the fourth player in league history to win the award unanimously. But that Irving received all but three first-place votes despite ranking 195th among 210 guards in defensive rating that season speaks volumes about the offensive focus of the media.

He did all the right things off the court along the way. He prayed to his departed mom before every game, and carried a Bible with his name embroidered on the cover with him on every road trip. The Good Book had been a gift from the mother of St. Patrick's teammate and best friend Jeremiah Green, whose enlarged heart had caused him to frighteningly collapse during a practice. Irving had carried Green to the sideline and accompanied him to the hospital.

Unlike some emerging superstars, Irving did not arrive at the arena with an entourage. He did not seek out a lucrative shoe deal or publicity that would further his brand. Irving the rookie had no brand—that would come later. After he nailed all eight of his three-point attempts to win Most Valuable Player honors at the Rising Stars Game during All-Star Weekend in Orlando, he insisted that the crystal with which he was presented did not obscure the "Cleveland" on his uniform as he was photographed. "That wasn't a publicity stunt at all," he said after the season. "I just wanted to make sure they got the Cleveland uniform in it. We're not as publicized as everybody else."

Was that sincerity or simply knowledge of how to win the affections of the public and organization? Some in the media that covered Irving and the Cavaliers believed he played them like a bass fiddle to place himself in a positive light and became more arrogant in time. Also concerning was that the team regressed in his rookie season, during which he ranked disturbingly in the bottom 4 percent of the NBA defensively. Irving allowed his opponents to shoot 48.3 percent from the field as the team lost twenty-eight of its final thirty-six games, including nineteen of the last twenty-four in which he played.

Cleveland Plain Dealer columnist Bill Livingston offered that Irving reminded him of the Cavaliers' onetime shooting guard World B. Free in that he had given the fan base a sense of hope. Free arrived at the tail end of the Ted Stepien era in the mid-1980s, brashly leading what had been a dysfunctional and horrible Cleveland team to the playoffs and playing perhaps the most significant role in saving it from ruin. The Cavaliers organization following the departure of James was certainly not in nearly as sorry condition as how Stepien left it. But Livingston believed that, just as Free had done, Irving was providing optimism. He also felt the team needed to hold Irving more accountable and that he should have worked to raise the level of production from his teammates.

"Kyrie was a better player than World, but he was also a guy that could make people come out," Livingston said. "Attendance stayed high because the fans sensibly felt that the franchise had been stabbed in the back by LeBron James. Kyrie gave them somebody to watch and look forward to see play. When he had that zero-assist game [in 2015] when LeBron came back, and LeBron took him aside and said this can't happen again, that was the type of player Kyrie was. He had a lot of freedom [before the return of James] because it was a bad team and he could pretty much do whatever he wanted. The Cavaliers had not had a strong coach. There weren't that many strong coaches in the NBA aside from [Gregg Popovich of San Antonio] and a few others because you have to keep the players happy. Kyrie has never been a good player in terms of making the team better."

He was that despite his talent as a ball handler and a finisher who was already second to none. He had proven as a mere rookie that he could score from anywhere on the court. He had established himself as lethal from beyond the arc. He could nail mid-range shots, banked or otherwise. He could fake defenders out of their jocks with his ballhandling and quick first step. He could weave his way through traffic and score on either side of the backboard with either hand from angles few others would even try, let alone drop through the hoop. He had shown that he could achieve as a scorer against the best in the world what he had already proven in lower levels of competition.

The Cavaliers needed his scoring. Their only other significant offensive threat was aging Antawn Jamison, a holdover from the first LeBron James era, whose acquisition was part of the last-ditch, desperate attempt to provide the superstar with the side talent to win a championship and keep him around—neither of which was accomplished. Now it would be up to Irving to lead a new contingent of Cavaliers to contention.

That did not happen. He received little help as the organization played the emerging game embraced by downtrodden franchises throughout the league that featured tanking, stockpiling high-draft picks, and shedding salary. But he also proved to be focused on ballhandling and scoring to the detriment of his defense and raising his all-around game to a level at which it would translate into more victories for Cleveland. One wondered if that would ever change.

5 Stagnation

The 2012 NBA playoffs were heating up. LeBron and the Heat were steam-rolling to the title. The ill-conceived prediction by Cavaliers owner Dan Gilbert that his team would win a crown before James did was about to be predictably proven wrong. His team was about as far removed from contention as any in the league, but Gilbert was waxing philosophic to the media about his plans to transform it from a bottom-feeder to a champion.

"We learn from everything we do, right decisions made, wrong decisions made, right strategies, wrong strategies, and you try to repeat the things you do right," Gilbert said. "We want to build a franchise with Kyrie or with other superstars—not around superstars. We think that's probably not a great formula for success or else we would have rings already here. We would have championship trophies. We believe 'the with' is the key here and we're looking forward to adding more great pieces."

Indeed, Gilbert's first attempt failed. The organization worked to surround James with enough veteran talent to claim a crown, most notably Larry Hughes, Mo Williams, and Shaquille O'Neal. But Hughes and Williams were good players, not great ones, and O'Neal was a superstar in name only, having long since left his prime. It seemed only through the tanking process and sawing off assets, which landed James in the first place, could the Cavaliers acquire enough talent through the draft and free agency to return to contention. Irving was the only major piece in place.

The NBA had always been to varying degrees a superstar-driven league. There had been Bill Russell and John Havlicek in Boston, Michael Jordan and Scottie Pippen in Chicago, and Kareem Abdul-Jabbar and Magic Johnson in Los Angeles. James had joined Miami to team up with All-Stars Dwyane Wade and Chris Bosh. Though there were exceptions—the Spurs won more through the embracing and executing of the Gregg Popovich system—it had become increasingly apparent (as the Golden State Warriors would later demonstrate) that superstars win championships.

It was hoped that the talent of Irving would eventually prove intriguing enough to pique the interest of premier free agents. That it would be LeBron James, who had just won his first NBA championship and had two years left on his contract with the Heat, remained a pipe dream at the time. But if James were to ever return to the Cavaliers, the idea of teaming up with Irving would have to inspire him. And the ice had begun to thaw. James had tweeted sentimentally about his days with the Cavaliers, and his loyalty to his hometown of Akron, just south of Cleveland, remained unshakable. He admitted a mistake with "The Decision," the nationally televised broadcast on ESPN in which he announced his departure from Cleveland and added that it would be great to come back. He had known Irving and Thompson since both were in high school. The former, in fact, had participated in the LeBron James Youth Basketball Camp at age 17. That James could opt out of his Heat contract in 2014 was not lost on the minds of the Cavaliers hierarchy. But they also knew that they had to make the team as attractive as possible for James or any prominent free agent seeking a shot at a championship.

Meanwhile, Irving was gearing up for his second season. His team had provided him with a backcourt mate in first-round pick and University of Syracuse shooting guard Dion Waiters. But the pair did not exactly go together like peanut butter and jelly. Neither was a traditional point guard who was willing to distribute the ball to open teammates, all of whom could have just as well converged to the basket for a possible offensive rebound, once either got the ball if they were not required to create space. Neither Irving nor Waiters were destined to give up possession. The offensive skills of both could have meshed wonderfully if they had shared the basketball and forced opponents to guard both of them on pick-and-rolls. But they performed less as teammates with common goals as individuals with personal motivations.

That Irving felt the need to serve almost exclusively as a scorer his rookie year given the dearth of offensive talent on the floor was understandable. The Cavaliers hoped that the addition of Waiters would convince Irving to gain a proper balance between scoring and distributing. But nothing changed.

"Kyrie was so supremely talented and confident in his ability that he had more confidence in himself taking shots than anyone else on the floor," said *Medina Gazette* reporter Noland. "That's not a horrible thing but as a point guard he's got to make sure his teammates get involved and there was a lot of watching him. Dion would take his turn making plays. Sometimes that worked and sometimes it was catastrophic. For the most part they operated independently of one another rather than making each other better."

What Irving did do was give the Cavaliers a closer with a killer attitude. One example occurred in late January with the team trailing Toronto by 2 points with twelve seconds remaining. Coach Byron Scott called timeout and instructed a clear-out for Irving. But rather than dissect the Raptors with his ankle-breaking ballhandling and drives to the basket, he pulled up and unloaded a three-pointer that dropped through the hole. Game. Set. Match. "Kyrie craved moments like that," Scott said.

Irving toiled tirelessly on his finishing. He would in practice encourage Shumpert to aggressively attempt to block his shots without warning to turn up the degree of difficulty and force him to drop the ball through the hoop from tougher angles. But the Cavaliers were forced to often operate independently due to Irving ailments. The list of injuries that have sidelined him throughout his career began before training camp in July, when during a practice in Las Vegas he broke his hand by slamming it in frustration against a wall after a turnover, an injury that required surgery. When asked about the impromptu manner and careless way in which Irving injured himself, Scott, who was still coach at the time, gave an impromptu answer. "Damn," he told the media. "Is that official enough for you?"

He then provided greater detail. "That was just something stupid on his part. I didn't see him initially hit the thing, but I saw when he came down the court he was kind of holding his hand. I said, 'What did you do?' The first thing he said was, 'Something stupid.' . . . He was upset with himself and he took it out on the wall. The wall won, obviously."

Irving returned in time for camp but was lost for a summer league period in which the intention was to gain an on-court familiarity with Waiters and fellow rookie Tyler Zeller. Irving was equally angry, as well as contrite. He stated his disappointment in himself and his need to become more responsible for his health. Though faultless, the injuries kept on coming. He lost three weeks in November to a fractured finger, then broke his nose his second game back, requiring him to wear a mask. The knee pain that remained a problem for years cost him twelve games later in the season. Coach Scott considered shutting him down in March, but Irving refused despite what had become the usual reality, that the team had long since been relegated to the role of spoiler.

By that time, Irving had become the seventh player in NBA history to earn an All-Star spot before his twenty-first birthday. He won the three-point contest the night before the annual showcase, then scored 15 points in the game. The mini-vacation for the rest of the league served to foment rumors that the talents of Irving had increased the chances of James returning after the following season. "He's unbelievable," said James, who spent much of the weekend watching and praising Irving. "He'll be [among] the top two, top three best point guards in the league. He's headed there already. He's doing some great things right now. They should be excited about having him in Cleveland."

Most premier athletes playing on poor teams in Cleveland and other secondary markets are consigned to comparative obscurity. Such was not the case with Irving, who received attention as a No. 1 overall pick trying, with understandably limited success, to replace James in the hearts and minds of Cavaliers fans. He launched his Uncle Drew character in May 2012 for Pepsi Max. The first video featured an aging, white-haired Irving schooling young ballers on a New Jersey playground and earning their respect. Uncle Drew started slowly on the court, missing shots and turning the ball over, but found his groove and began draining three-pointers and driving lay-ups to the joy of his fellow competitors and a growing number of curious attendees.

A whirlwind of All-Star weekend activity placed Irving squarely in the spotlight. He was among the players asked to shoot a segment with hip-hop artist will.i.am pegged for use during the playoffs and 2013–14 regular season. He engaged in a dancing competition. He spoke about his obligation to community service. And he answered all the questions about the possible return of James. That was certainly the most popular subject on the mind of the media.

"It's funny how the roles have changed a little bit," Irving said. "I was replacing [James], and now there's all these rumors that he can come back. But it's about brushing off that question and just being in the present—just being in the present and trying to develop this core group for the Cavaliers. My eventual goal is to win a championship. And before I retire I just want to win a championship. That's it. It's a learning process game to game."

One can only speculate on his thoughts at the time about playing along-side James, which he understood would downgrade him to second fiddle. Had he yet to formulate in his heart and mind the notion that he could grow into being the leader, the premier player, on an NBA championship team? Though the 2013 Cavaliers certainly did not boast the talent to contend, his all-around performance on the court screamed out that he had a long way to go and required a dramatic shift in mind-set on the defensive end to reach that level.

Meanwhile, his Cavaliers were regressing. Despite an 11-9 March, they finished at 24-58, a worse winning percentage than they managed in Irving's rookie year. They lost twenty of their last twenty-four games, due greatly to an Irving-Waiters backcourt that consistently rolled out red carpets to the hoop and left shooters open enough to scan the crowd for hecklers. The human sieves constituted one of the worst starting backcourts in basketball defensively. Irving ranked 169th among 207 NBA guards with a defensive rating of 107.7 while Waiters placed 188th at 109.4.

On the surface, Irving performed well offensively. He scored 22.5 points per game, which would remain his highest until the 2016–17 season, his last in Cleveland. He averaged 5.9 assists per game, a comparatively low number for a point guard, but a slight increase over his rookie year. But his shooting accuracy decreased from two- and three-point range, as well as at the line, and his turnovers increased. More telling is that he ranked just 90th among all NBA guards in offensive rating, which even placed him well behind Waiters.

Irving had become more of a prolific scorer, but he was stagnating as a player on a horrible team. He could draw gasps from crowds and television audiences with his ballhandling magic and fantastic finishes. He had gained a deserved reputation as a player unafraid of the moment with battles hanging in the balance. He ranked first in the NBA in what 82games.com called "clutch time statistics" by scoring 53.8 points and shooting 54.4 percent from the field per forty-eight minutes in games with scores within 5 points with less than five minutes left. Only 19 percent of his clutch-time shots were assisted, proving his willingness to take charge with victories on the line. But he was an enigma in sneakers. He was supposed to be the straw that stirred the drink, yet Cleveland performed worse than it had his rookie season. Certainly, the list of players in basketball history who could transform a team into a contender single-handedly is short. Irving was not expected to be a LeBron James, Michael Jordan or Kareem Abdul-Jabbar. But a player with his talent was counted upon to at least send the Cavaliers in a positive direction.

The team struggles did not sit well with Gilbert, who had left open the possibility that it could earn a playoff spot despite Scott's warning that the Cavaliers were quite distant from reaching that status. Though Scott had admonished Irving about his defense, he had gained a reputation in previous stints as more of an offensive coach. The Cavaliers ranked twenty-seventh of thirty teams defensively that year. And since effectiveness on that side of the court is based on intensity, desire, and attention to detail, particularly considering the young athleticism of players such as Irving, Waiters, and Tristan Thompson, it could be surmised that the Cavaliers lacked motivation to improve in that area.

Had all the losing caused the defensive malaise? Or had the defensive malaise caused all the losing? After all, the Cavaliers ranked near the middle of the pack in offensive efficiency. Yet they sported one of the worst records in the NBA. It had become painfully obvious that the main issue was defense. It had become equally obvious that it would not improve unless Irving and Waiters made it a priority. And that was not about to happen.

Not even with a new coach and, for the Cavaliers, an old coach. Soon after Irving's second season had concluded, Gilbert fired Scott and replaced him with Mike Brown, who had coached the team for six years during the first LeBron James era. He had guided the Cavaliers to their first NBA Finals in 2007 and what remain the two best regular season records in their history. The team was among the stingiest in the league during that stretch. Gilbert had expressed disappointment over the lack of progress the Cavaliers had made defensively and cited that as the motivation of his move.

"To me, it just fits perfect like a puzzle," said Gilbert, who admitted to having erred when he fired Brown following the departure of James. "It all comes together, Mike Brown what he brings is exactly what the franchise needs right now. We need an authentic, hard-working grinder who is a defensive-first coach who is engaged at all levels at all times."

But for Brown the Grinder to fix the defense he would require players who would grind along with him. Irving and Waiters continued grinding individually on offense, often to the detriment of the team. A turbulent third season for Irving was about to begin. And its aftermath would prove profoundly impactful to his life and career.

6 Old Story and New Contract

The plan wasn't working. And that was to build the Cavaliers through high draft picks and shed cap space to lure premier free agents to Cleveland. One hand would wash the other. The brilliant young talent procured through the draft would convince seekers of championships to sign. One player who famously sought teams that could win titles, of course, was LeBron James.

But there was no brilliant young talent aside from the one-dimensional Irving. Dion Waiters, the top choice in 2012, did not mesh well with him. Though offensively explosive and improving on defense, he had proven himself inconsistent and self-centered on the court. Waiters, however, was not as big a disaster as 2013 first overall pick Anthony Bennett. In what was generally accepted as a weak draft class, the Cavaliers passed on future stars Victor Oladipo and the insanely athletic "Greek Freak" Giannis Antetokounmpo to select Bennett, the burly UNLV power forward. Bennett flopped miserably. His lack of talent, work ethic, and conditioning added up to a miserable rookie season. He played just one awful season with the Cavaliers, and he left the NBA after stints with four teams and just four starts in four years.

Meanwhile, the contentious relationship between Irving and Waiters continued to disintegrate. Waiters denied any issue, but a report circulated by ESPN and former Cavaliers beat writer Chris Broussard claimed that the team was seeking to trade Waiters and that Irving called a players-only team meeting in late November 2013 after a 29-point loss at Minnesota lowered the team's record to 3-6. Wrote Broussard:

> Irving called the meeting after the game, and every player spoke. When Waiters was given the floor, he criticized [Tristan] Thompson and Irving, accusing them of playing "buddy ball" and often refusing to pass to him. Thompson took umbrage with Waiters' words and went back at him verbally. The two confronted each other, but teammates intervened before it could escalate into a fight.
>
> However, Waiters and Irving are not close. Waiters believes the Cavaliers have a double standard when it comes to Irving, sources said. Waiters feels that while Irving is allowed to get away with loafing defensively, making turnovers and taking bad shots, he is taken out of games for such things. Waiters has shared his views with Brown and [general manager Chris Grant]

The claim that the confrontation became physical gained credence when Irving arrived to the Friday night game with a black eye and broken nose while Waiters missed the next two days with what was officially announced as an illness. Waiters insisted that the meeting was not marred by such an occurrence, but rumors persisted. Waiters was soon removed from the starting lineup in favor of Matthew Dellavedova, a scrappy, but athletically challenged off-guard who played tenacious defense and certainly fit the grinder mold Brown preferred. Yet the losing continued. The Cavaliers dropped six of seven after the team meeting and eventually plummeted to 16-33, at which time Gilbert fired Grant and named Griffin the acting general manager.

Irving and the Cavaliers bottomed out in a pathetic home loss to the terrible Lakers that precipitated the shakeup. The team had already lost five consecutive games when they fell behind by 29 points, prompting boos from the crowd and motivating Brown to remove Irving and three other starters in the fourth quarter. Most embarrassing was that the Lakers played the last few minutes with just five healthy players. One remained on the court after fouling out because coach Mike D'Antoni had nobody else available.

The front office had tried desperately and a bit recklessly around midseason to transform the Cavaliers into a contender to no avail. They gave up five draft picks for accomplished forward Luol Deng and offensiveminded center Spencer Hawes, both of whom could bolt in free agency following the season. Neither acquisition had the desired effect nor did they make any commitment to staying in Cleveland.

Meanwhile, the Brown emphasis on defense simply wasn't getting through to Irving, who finished the season fourth-last in defensive rating among all NBA guards that played at least thirty-five minutes per game. Even his offense trended downward despite the defensive attention given to the likes of Waiters, Deng, and Hawes. Irving shot just a career-low 43 percent from the field and bottomed out at under 36 percent from three-point range.

Though the team finally righted itself in winning 17 of 33 down the stretch, Irving and his father Drederick, whose opinions he valued more than any other, had serious reservations about the direction of the franchise. That alarmed Griffin and Brown. Brown favored dealing Irving in the knowledge that a bounty of talent could be acquired in return, but Griffin wanted Irving to stick around. The organization ruled out a trade and set its sights on convincing Irving to sign an extension. Such was a tall task given a relationship between Brown and Irving that seemed irreparable. But that became a moot point in May when Gilbert fired Brown after just one season and retained Griffin as the full-time general manager.

A more mature Irving admitted four years later a sense of regret for how he treated Brown. Asked about their initial relationship as the finalsbound Cavaliers prepared to face the Warriors, with whom Brown had landed a job as an assistant coach, Irving called it a learning experience. "I was a 21-year-old kid, just trying to lead a franchise, and he was a new head coach that I had to get introduced to a new offense, new players, as well as a new system," Irving said. "I kind of regret being part of that, because he was just trying to teach me a lot of things that I didn't necessarily understand as a 21-year-old in the NBA."

The departure of Brown and permanent promotion of Griffin, altered the organizational mind-set about Irving's future in Cleveland. Griffin worked to improve the relationship between Irving and the team. He maintained contact with the point guard during the search for Brown's replacement, which resulted in the surprising hire of American-born David Blatt, who had enjoyed great success coaching internationally. Griffin eagerly got the disgruntled player acquainted with Blatt, as well as new assistant Tyronn Lue, who had been strongly considered for the head coaching job and, as a former NBA point guard, certainly had something in common with Irving and was pegged as a mentor. Even Griffin's background proved a positive influence in convincing Irving to stay. The general manager had served for seventeen years with a Phoenix Suns organization that stressed high-powered, fast-paced offensive basketball. One and all made it clear to Irving that improvement on that side of the court would be a strong focus going forward.

The Cavaliers boasted $20 million in cap space heading into the 2014 off-season. But they understood the importance of keeping Irving, whose extension would not take hold for another year. There would normally have been no rush—the deadline for an agreement was not until the end of October. But though the possibility of landing James had been played out in the media, the organization had not been informed of his intentions. Griffin and Gilbert set their sights on Irving.

The multi-million-dollar question that has been asked and never answered by Irving, though future events certainly provided an indication of his mind-set, is whether he wanted James to return. A year after Irving demanded a trade in 2017 that landed him in Boston and revealed an apparent dissatisfaction over playing second fiddle to arguably the greatest player in NBA history, Griffin stated that the point guard had a different plan in 2014. Irving had recruited restricted free agent Gordon

Hayward to sign an offer sheet with the Cavaliers. Though considered an up-and-comer who had improved his scoring average every season, Hayward was coming off his worst season as a shooter and had been one of the few guards shackled with a worse defensive rating than Irving. The plan also included signing veteran swingman Trevor Ariza and forward/center Channing Frye, who could stretch the floor with his range.

Irving would have to wait a couple of years to play with Frye in Cleveland and until 2017 to join Hayward in Boston. And he already made his feelings known about sharing the court with James, according to *Akron Beacon Journal* beat reporter Jason Lloyd, who has since joined the online news site the Athletic Cleveland. "It has been made clear to me by multiple people, Kyrie never really wanted LeBron to come back [to Cleveland] in the first place," Lloyd said. "He didn't think it was necessary. LeBron said something to Kyrie on the court following a game when he was with Miami . . . to the effect of, 'Keep going, keep doing what you're doing. You never know, I could be back here one day.' And Kyrie basically said, 'What's he talking about; we don't need him.'"

The scenario that played out might have indeed taken a different turn had Irving known that James would soon be wearing a Cleveland uniform again. But even the Cavaliers had no idea that James would be back. They hoped to make him an offer if he indeed opted to test the free-agent waters, but they did not believe they could land him. The final push to sign Irving to a new contract began immediately after the team had made official the hiring of coaches Blatt and Lue. The two joined Gilbert, Griffin, and minority owners Jeff Cohen and Nate Forbes in a midnight dinner in a private room of an Italian restaurant in Manhattan on July 1, 2014. They met Irving, his father, and agent Jeff Wechsler, and offered a five-year $90 million contract, stressing that changes were coming. According to Griffin, the possibility of bringing James back to the team was never mentioned. But the brass sought to convince Irving that they were pursuing other major free agents. Irving soon agreed to sign the extension.

And to prove they weren't just blowing smoke the Cavaliers had already begun contacting Hayward and talented free agent forward Chandler

Parsons. Ariza and Frye were also on their call list. They quickly scheduled a meeting with Hayward, who would start at small forward alongside a backcourt that featured Irving at the point and coveted, super-athletic first overall draft pick Andrew Wiggins at shooting guard. Gilbert flew to Hayward's hometown of Indianapolis and was prepared to offer him a four-year deal that started at $15 million for the upcoming season. But on that fateful day Griffin received a phone call from James representative Rich Paul, who confirmed that his client was indeed no lock to return to Miami and would be meeting with potential suitors over the next few days in his Cleveland office. So much for the offer to Hayward. In the time it takes to pick up a phone and listen to a few words, everything had changed for Irving, Hayward, Wiggins, the franchise, and its fans. Irving had already signed his contract. There was nothing he could do. The most exciting, rewarding journey in Cavaliers history was about to launch. One could certainly speculate that a team featuring Irving, Hayward, and Wiggins would have vaulted the team into the playoffs, but not title contention.

Irving did not hint at any regret after James announced his return in a *Sports Illustrated* essay that inspired celebration throughout northeast Ohio. But one could interpret his verbal reaction as a bit muted. If Irving was indeed irked that the man known as The King had made Quicken Loans Arena his royal palace once again, he could not have expressed it two days after signing a five-year extension. That would have made him look petulant. The bottom line in the minds of most was that the Cavaliers had been rotten since Irving arrived in the NBA and were about to be transformed into one of the premier teams in the league, perhaps even the title favorite. How they would have fared with Hayward, Ariza, Frye, Wiggins, and possibly Parsons in the fold can only be imagined, but it's hard to believe that that group would have reached one NBA Final, let alone four in a row.

No matter the scenario that would have played out, Irving was all sweetness and light when James revealed the news that placed him back into revered status among Cleveland fans. He just called the signing of James "exciting," whereas words such as "wonderful" or "great" would have indicated a more positive feeling. Heck, a tornado is "exciting."

"I'm glad we got it done," Irving said of his new contract. "A couple days later, [James] decided to come back to Cleveland. The rest is history. Now, we'll let [general manager] David Griffin do his thing.... We wanted to make it as easy as possible. I wanted to show my commitment to them and they wanted to show their commitment to me. That's what it was really about. They wanted me to be a part of their future. It's a huge monkey off my back, with all the speculation and all the B.S. I was hearing. I'm just happy I got it out of the way."

The reference to Griffin was in regard to future free-agent signings that included the Timberwolves versatile and talented power forward Kevin Love, who would cost Wiggins and serve as the third in the triumvirate of All-Stars that James and the Cavaliers, following the Heat philosophy, deemed necessary to win a championship. Love thrived both as a post-up player and three-point shooter and had established himself as one of the premier rebounders in the sport.

James, who is renowned for his research into and knowledge of his fellow NBA players past and present, had grown quite familiar with the talents of Irving. He had dropped hints while with Miami at his consideration of coming home through compliments of the young point guard. But he had little personal contact with Irving prior to their first workouts with the Cavaliers. They had shared the court for Team USA in 2012, but Irving styled his game and embraced the same motivations, not with James but with his idol Kobe Bryant.

Irving saw the man in the mirror as an individual killer of defenders rather than a point guard who, through ball and player movement and precision passes, could raise the level of teammate performance. James could destroy opponents in isolation as well, especially by bullying them in post-ups, but his priority was the involvement of all wearing the same uniform. He took pride in the capability of playing any position on the court but had proven himself arguably more effective as a traditional point guard than any other spot. Irving boasted the talent of a distributor, but neither the mind-set nor desire to be one.

As for his embracing of the "mamba mentality—the killer instinct—that defined Bryant, there was something missing. *Medina Gazette* beat writer Noland perceived a significant difference. "It's a far-fetched comparison," he said. "Number one, Kobe is six foot six and could guard a lot more guys. He was a tenacious defender for the bulk of his career. He would play as hard on that end of the floor as he did on the other end and we all know how hard he played on that end. Offensively, there were some similarities. Neither of them met a shot they didn't like and both of them were completely willing and wanted to take the big shot no matter the situation and how they'd played up to that point in a game. Both of them wanted the ball in their hands and were willing to be the hero and equally willing to be the goat."

Indeed, the 2013–14 Cavaliers allowed 106.8 points per 100 possessions with Irving on the floor and just 101.4 points with him on the bench. But it would not be his defense that rankled James the most about Irving. Over the next several years, after all, James too would often save his energy by loafing on that end of the court as the Cavaliers of the post-Brown era would give opponents the red-carpet treatment to the basket or leave shooters wide open on the perimeter. What irked James far more was the unwillingness of Irving to utilize the offensive talents of his teammates. James could not understand why a brilliant ball handler and capable passer such as Irving, who attracted so much defensive attention and boasted a bevy of open shooters and teammates slashing to the basket, could average only 5 assists per game and sometimes hardly racked up any. One might argue that Irving was so focused on his ballhandling and his defender that his court vision outside the realm of that one-on-one battle suffered, but that was certainly not a fatal flow. He just showed little motivation to change.

That was a flaw James could not tolerate. He yearned to be a father figure, or at least a big brother, to the still-young Irving, whose love and respect for his real dad would not allow James too significant an influence in his basketball-related mind-set and desires. That the Cavaliers would emerge as a title contender with James, Irving, and Love on the same team was a given. Just how effectively they would mesh remained to be seen.

One thing became apparent immediately. Irving was too strong-willed to accept drastic alterations in his own game. His assist totals were about to drop despite the additions of James and Love and his defensive intensity was going to remain a concern.

7 Changing Expectations

One might have figured that Kyrie Irving needed far more exposure to big games. His Cavaliers, after all, had not exactly been the focus of attention since he had arrived. They had owned the worst record in the NBA since LeBron James bolted for Miami. They had never sniffed a playoff chase. And the All-Star Game certainly does not qualify as pressure basketball. Individual defense in that annual exhibition is a wave, smile, and red carpet to the hoop.

The return of The King to Cleveland was destined to turn up the heat on Irving. His team was about to be a regular on nationally televised games and expected to extend deep into the postseason. Most considered the Cavaliers immediate favorites to win a weak Eastern Conference. So it was believed that Irving's participation in the FIBA World Cup in the late summer before training camp would provide him experience in spotlighted events. The tournament that is played every four years has proven difficult for the Americans, even after NBA players began participating in 1994, as the premier opponents from other nations began to catch up. The host U.S. team finished a woeful sixth in 2002 and failed to reach the finals in 2006.

The 2014 World Cup promised no dominance. That was especially true considering the NBA players that begged off participation, including James, Kobe Bryant, Chris Paul, and Kevin Durant. But Irving, reunited with Duke coach Mike Krzyzewski, played a huge role in breaking that promise. His team won all nine games by an average of 33 points and none by less than 21. Included was a 96–68 victory over Lithuania in the semifinal, in which Irving led the team with 18 points and 4 assists, and a 129–92 rout of Serbia in which he nailed all six of his three-point attempts and tallied 26 points to clinch Most Valuable Player honors for the event. Irving had risen to the occasion on a big stage—it certainly would not be the last time.

But he was jolted back to reality as training camp began. His Cavaliers had only once won more than three games in a row—let alone nine—and he and his teammates had plenty of work to do with a new coach and revamped roster. Expectations were about to change drastically for Irving and the Cavs. "For the first time," said Griffin, "he really had to learn what it took to be successful. He had never been in a situation where the expectation was excellence every day. Even at Duke, he only played 11 games."

The focus to transforming arguably the finest individual talent in franchise history into its first champion became a bit blurred when Waiters stated two weeks before the regular season, and despite seemingly strong evidence to the contrary, that he and Irving constituted the greatest starting backcourt in the league. That declaration raised the ire of Washington Wizards guard Bradley Beal, who had made an identical claim about him and John Wall. Other backcourt standouts, such as emerging Warriors superstar Steph Curry, soon chimed in. Statistical comparisons showed the Irving-Waiters backcourt significantly behind those of Wall and Beal, Kyle Lowry and DeMar DeRozan (Toronto), Curry and Klay Thompson (Golden State), and Eric Bledsoe and Goran Dragic (Phoenix), both offensively and defensively.

But there was intention behind the claim. Waiters used the braggadocio to unite a relationship with Irving that had been so strained the previous season that a players-only meeting had been deemed necessary to address their issues. Waiters spoke of a new, positive vibe in the locker room. James offered his hope that Waiters and Irving could complement each other on the court rather than drag the team down with selfishness and ball-hogging. Irving would be tested. He thrived in the half-court, dribbling on the perimeter while eyeing his defender, looking for an opening, and faking him out of his jock on the way to a breathtaking finish. Now he would be asked to play the point on a fast-break offense that utilized the immense open-court talents of James and allow Love to find a free spot to shoot before the defense could adjust or find quick post-up positions down low. Irving was expected to be a pass-first point guard—which is like asking a cat to bark. A style based on attacking in isolation had been ingrained in Irving since his days going one-on-one with Drederick in the driveway. He was never going to be transformed into a Rajon Rondo or Chris Paul. And he and Waiters would never find a way to play together effectively and selflessly.

That became apparent early in the regular season as the Cavaliers embarked on Game 3 on a short western swing. They were outscored in the final three quarters by Portland, 70–48, as Irving shot 3-of-17 and combined with Waiters to hit just 6-of-28. The inaccuracy did not motivate either to shy away from jacking up shots and destroying any offensive flow. A discouraged James stood in the corner, going scoreless and taking just four shots after halftime, as the backcourt mates refused to pass him or anyone else the ball. James finished with 11 points, his lowest single-game total in nearly six years, and he spoke after the game about the need to break bad habits cemented over two seasons, obviously referring to Irving and Waiters.

James was in a quandary. He could eschew a team style that seemed impossible to achieve with the two starting guards jacking up shot after shot and try to win games with his own aggressiveness. Or he could continue to show tough love and work to change the mind-sets of Irving and Waiters by setting up teammates and refusing to play their selfishness game. He toyed with the notion that winning at that stage of team growth was less important than developing the right habits. James understood that it was all on his shoulders. He had to teach them. LeBron James University was open for business. And it was up to Irving and Waiters to soak in his lessons.

Waiters dropped out immediately. Removed from the starting lineup for a game the next night in Utah, he bolted to the locker room during the national anthem. Though he continued to receive significant minutes, he remained a substitute until the Cavaliers dispatched him to Oklahoma City in early January. The benching of Waiters helped free up Irving to take 23 shots and score 34 points in a loss to the Jazz that was secured, ironically, by a Gordon Hayward buzzer-beater. But it was another statistic that irked James. That was Irving's assist total, one that could be found in the middle of a doughnut.

James confronted his teammate, who was contrite. "He came up to me and was like, 'One, you can never have another game with no assists. You can damn near have just one, two, three, but you can't have zero,'" Irving reported. "And I was like, 'All right, cool, it won't happen again.'"

It certainly didn't happen again. The Cavaliers thrived that season when Irving showed a willingness to distribute. He managed just five games with double-figure dimes (that is, assists) in the regular season and playoffs combined, and the team won all of them by an average of 14.4 points. Most impressive was that the Cavaliers outscored their opponents by 106 points in those victories while Irving was on the court.

But the fans and media paid little attention to such statistics. After all, this was an era in which player motivation leaned toward landing a spot on the ESPN "SportsCenter" Top 10 highlights. Irving grabbed that spotlight with overwhelming offensive performances, twice exceeding 50 points. He overcame a 0-for-7 start in a revenge battle against Portland to nail 11 three-pointers and finish with a career-high 55 in a close win that was achieved without James, who was sidelined with a sprained wrist. Irving, who had recently missed time with back tightness, scored twice in the last 75 seconds to polish off the Blazers. After Irving clinched the win with the last of his points, James sprinted over to greet him. Irving downplayed his heroics, speaking instead about the importance of a winning streak that had reached eight games and would eventually extend to twelve. But James opted instead to celebrate the enormity of the achievement, tweeting: "Just watched live one of if not the greatest performances by a person and he happens to be my teammate/runningmate/brother Kyrie Irving."

The significance of the tear was not lost on Irving as it related to the Cavaliers and especially Coach Blatt, whose repeated claims that he had proven himself highly accomplished despite having never coached in the NBA had grated on his players. Blatt repeatedly associated winning internationally with career accomplishments equal to that of the premier NBA coaches. Such claims might have been given greater credence had the Cavaliers performed to the level of their talent. But a six-game losing streak in early January had dropped them shockingly to under .500 at midseason. It appeared that a team considered the likely Eastern Conference finals representative might struggle simply to earn a playoff spot. And Blatt was not exactly receiving glowing praise from James, whose lukewarm support coincided with reports that the coach could be on the verge of losing his job. Irving was not one to be critical. "I would do anything for Coach Blatt," he said.

Many in the Cleveland media believed that Irving gave stock answers rather than truly revealing his inner thoughts and feelings. Among them was longtime *Medina Gazette* reporter Noland. "I oftentimes walked away questioning the authenticity of his cooperation with the media, especially when there were cameras around," Noland said. "The cameras came on and the smiling face would come up and he would give lazy answers. . . . I always walked away with the impression that when we turned our backs on him, he was probably thinking to himself, 'That will be enough to keep those schmucks happy for another day.'"

Those schmucks and everyone else that witnessed it were certainly impressed when Irving shattered the personal scoring record he had set six weeks earlier. He buried the Spurs—in San Antonio, no less—with a 57-point outburst that keyed an overtime victory in which he rewrote the record books. It remained through 2018 the highest point total of a

James teammate. It shattered the franchise single-game scoring mark. And it was the most points scored against a defending NBA champion since the immortal Wilt Chamberlain tallied 62 against Boston in 1962.

Irving tossed in everything but the kitchen sink, then added the kitchen sink. He befuddled defenders with his ballhandling and buried them with his marksmanship. He drained a three-pointer to chop the Cleveland deficit to 110–107 with thirty-one seconds left, then nailed an off-balance bomb over premier defensive guard Kawhi Leonard to tie it. He then dominated overtime, scoring 11 points to clinch a signature conquest in which he hit 20 of 32 shots from the field, including all seven from beyond the arc.

The triumph proved significant beyond its place in the win column. It highlighted a blossoming of the on-court relationship between Irving and James, who had scored 31 points in the game. And the Cavaliers had won 23 of their last 28. Most important was that after a morose and stunningly underachieving first half to the season, they were finally enjoying playing together. The defeat of powerful San Antonio on its court was a sweet example. "It was such a fun game," Irving said. "The crowd was into it. They sold out, they came to see a great game and it was. Once Bron gets into those step-back threes, we were just looking at each other, 'Man this is just so much fun.'"

Indeed, they had come a long way. The two stars had been sparkling in distant galaxies earlier in the year. James had usurped much of the ballhandling duties. Both players thrived in isolation. Irving was unaccustomed to playing without the ball, but he often watched as James dribbled at the top of the key and made his move with time running off the shot clock. The difference was that James was most often looking to find an open teammate or cutter. Irving's offensive game was based on playing one-on-one with the ball, not finding open space on the court. And when he did handle the ball, he often frustrated James, Love, and his other teammates. Irving was a black hole. Once he got possession, they were needed only to crash the boards for a possible offensive rebound.

That never changed. The theories are many as to why his assist totals remained stagnant despite sharing the court with James and Love. That

James took assist opportunities away was a factor. But some might believe he lacked confidence as a passer. Or that he felt the best opportunity to score points for his team was to finish the play himself. Or that he was simply selfish—that he embraced individual rather than team achievements to a far greater degree. That question has never been answered and strengthens the enigmatic side of Kyrie Irving. No matter the reasons for his refusal to alter his offensive mind-set. James understood and appreciated his talents, so as the season progressed he worked hard to develop as strong a chemistry with Irving as possible, accepted him as an untraditional point guard, and simply let him do his thing.

The greatest adjustments made by Irving, though never fully, as would be proven in time, were mental and emotional. He was no longer the center of the Cleveland basketball universe. It mattered not that he scored 112 points in two games combined. It didn't matter what he accomplished on the court. He was forced to come to grips with the reality that he played second fiddle to James and would always play second fiddle to James. Such is the lot in life of any player who wears the same uniform. The best Irving could hope for would be serving as a Scottie Pippen to a Michael Jordan. There was no room on the throne for anyone but The King. Teammates such as wise veteran Mike Miller, with whom he spent much time on the road, helped Irving make progress in his on-court relationship with James, and the Cavaliers benefited greatly. An appreciative Irving even presented the shoes he wore in his 57-point game to Miller, complete with autograph and date. But one could only predict that Irving would never embrace—or even accept—the role of Robin to that of Batman.

Or Dick Grayson to that of Bruce Wayne. Irving did not want to be a youthful ward or even a little brother. James yearned to impart his vast wisdom about the game onto his younger teammate. Irving could not have at his disposal a more willing wealth of knowledge than the man generally accepted as a basketball genius. Irving was an instinctive player. James was a thinker, a strategist. The older man had also gained experience in the game of life for NBA players. Irving talked a good game about gaining insight from James. He even strengthened his work ethic in practice to earn trust—and James noticed the difference.

"LeBron's view of things has changed because he's no longer . . . looking across the locker room and asking, 'Does this guy have my back?' or 'Is this guy my brother?'" Irving said. "When we came into the locker room last year, it would probably be about the performance I had, in a selfish way. Because, you know, you become a losing team, you build bad habits. . . . It doesn't matter that he's older. I've been playing against older guys my whole entire life. I mean, I played with my dad in New York City against older guys all the time. I feel like I have an old-school game. I do things people probably think a 23-year-old shouldn't know to do. I have that in my game from my dad and from working hard. And LeBron has a lot of things that he has developed, and I want to learn, too."

The Cavaliers took their momentum from their twelve-game winning streak and ran with it. They did not lose two straight games through the second half of the year until an April 12 loss to Boston in which James, Irving, and Love all rested. Blatt sat his premier players periodically to ensure health heading into the playoffs. The top seed proved unattainable anyway—surprising Atlanta owned that. The Cavaliers had finished the regular season on a 34-9 run and owned a 53-29 record.

Irving was about to embark on a new adventure. He understood that the NBA playoffs are a different animal, but it must be experienced for the intensity it requires to be fully appreciated. It is more than the second season. It is *the* season for teams such as the Cavaliers with title expectations. And when the Celtics came to town for a first-round battle, Irving wasted no time proving himself ready to rise to the occasion.

8 The Ecstasy and the Agony

It was the moment for mamba mentality. The playoffs. A time for a killer instinct that requires aggressiveness and self-assurance. Those were traits that Drederick Irving had drilled into his son a decade earlier. And it was that same mamba mentality that Lakers isolation assassin Kobe Bryant inspired the younger Irving to embrace.

The date was April 19, 2015. The site was Quicken Loans Arena. The victim was the overmatched Boston Celtics. Those that thought Irving would be overwhelmed by the pressure of playing his first postseason game had another think coming. He professed a case of nerves before battle, but they didn't show from tip-off forward. He displayed his full arsenal, mesmerizing and splitting multiple defenders with his quickness and ballhandling wizardry, then finishing at the rim from unimaginable angles. He hit mid-range jumpers. He drained deep bombs. Irving was the Swiss Army knife of scoring. After hitting the Celtics with drives to the hoop early, forcing the defense to guard against penetration, he nailed four three-pointers in the second quarter and finished with 30 points on 11-of-21 shooting.

Irving played his part of a Big Three machine that the organization dreamed about when they signed James and Love but it was one that rarely ran on all cylinders during the regular season. The trio combined for 69 points. The most impressive given his age and inexperience in the playoffs was Irving, who had praised Celtics guard Avery Bradley as his toughest defender in a question-and-answer session with kids before the season, then schooled him in the playoff opener. And following the victory Irving expressed pride in how his All-Star teammates had performed.

"Obviously we've all accomplished a lot," he said. "As you prepare and get ready for the postseason, you want your best players to be at their best. We set the tone at both ends of the floor. We set it mentally and physically. We want to be there for everyone. We have to hold each other accountable. We got together, we were the Big Three. We have a lot of really great players on this team, but we set the tone."

What Irving could not have anticipated was that the physical issues that had sidelined him on occasion in the regular season, as well as a sickening injury to Love, were about to destroy his dreams of a crown, as well as those of his team and their title-starved city. The seeds of disappointment were planted in Game 3 against Boston when Irving sprained his right foot, causing a poor effort in which he hit just 3 of 11 shots. Meanwhile, the Celtics had begun to show frustration as they toiled in vain to avoid a sweep. In the first quarter of the clincher, Kelly Olynyk yanked down so hard on Love's arm that it resulted in a dislocated shoulder and a one-game suspension for the Celtic center. The Big Three was down to the Big Two. And Irving would never be 100 percent again through the playoff run, admitting that he had lost a bit of his acceleration.

The good news initially was that the blitz of Boston provided the Cavaliers an eight-day break in which to nurse their wounds and prepare for a second-round matchup against much-tougher Chicago. Irving tallied 30 in the opener, but his offensive production was nearly matched by Bulls point guard Derrick Rose. Neither Irving nor his teammates could keep up with Rose. Despite the significant scoring output, Irving finished the game with a negative 14 plus-minus that doubled the margin of defeat. He was beaten off the dribble at times and struggled defending the pick-and-roll against Rose, who often found teammate Pau Gasol for open shots and easy baskets.

Having lost home-court advantage, the Cavaliers bounced back to win Game 2, but Irving's right foot did not bounce back two nights later. That is when he reinjured it in a 99–96 defeat that threatened to push his team to the brink of elimination. Adding insult to the injury to Irving, Rose scored 30 and banked in an off-balance, desperation game-winning three-pointer. Irving hit just three of 13 shots, recorded zero assists for the first time since James lambasted him for it in Utah, and finished with the worst plus-minus of anyone in the game at negative 8. He struggled offensively and defensively. He had an easy out as the media approached—but he refused to take it. It took Blatt to let the cat out of the bag, though the cat's head was certainly showing. After all, Irving spent some of the night limping around the court. He tried to hide the injury so the Bulls wouldn't attack him on their offensive end.

"I kept it to myself, kept it within the team," Irving said. "I understand what Coach Blatt was doing to protect me, but I just wanted to play through it. There's no excuse for myself. . . . You try not to limp, you try not to let anyone know. [But] we're at the highest level. There are no secrets. It's just part of the game. For me, as a prideful man, I just want to go out there and compete with my brothers."

His brothers watched him hobble and shoot 2-for-10 in Game 4 with just two assists. Irving was so compromised defensively that he had been subbed out by scrappy Matthew Dellavedova when Rose again tied it with a late shot. Blatt nearly committed the faux pas of the ages when he tried to call a time-out the Cavaliers didn't have, only to be held back by Lue. That merely gave James less confidence in his coach than he had displayed much of the year and so did the coach's play call with the season teetering on the brink. Blatt designed one for Irving that James nixed in favor of one for himself in which he would fake a drive and shoot a jumper. James drilled it at the buzzer to give his team the victory and perhaps save the season as well as, quite conceivably, Blatt's job.

What it seemed could not be saved was Irving's health. He underwent an MRI on his knee that came back negative, but it still caused him pain. He had played forty minutes in the win, which didn't provide it the necessary rest. The diagnosis did inspire Irving to play more aggressively and with greater confidence in scoring 23 points in Game 5, but Lady Luck proved to be an enemy in the clincher when he landed on Tristan Thompson's foot and tweaked his knee again.

Irving played only three of the last eighteen minutes in a victory in the Eastern Conference finals opener in Atlanta, then missed the next two games as the Cavaliers continued to outclass the Hawks. Blatt called it pain management. But *Cleveland Plain Dealer* beat writer Joe Vardon years later reported that James believed the issue to be more a pain in the butt. James didn't feel that Irving should have been missing in action. "This annoyed LeBron and LeBron's people to no end," Vardon told sports talk radio station 92.3 The Fan in Cleveland. "They were calling him soft and questioning his toughness, and LeBron was doing it in comments to the media."

Such criticism was certainly not made public and Irving's knee and foot injuries were no phantoms. But aches and pains after a hundred games are a given for all NBA players. Irving stressed to reporters the need to play through pain in the playoffs but had done so only sporadically. That he was sidelined for Games 2 and 3 with a finals berth hanging in the balance could have irked teammates and several team officials who, according to Vardon, offered their belief before those games that Irving would be on the court, only to be proven wrong. Among those who spoke up was swingman Iman Shumpert, who expressed his view without calling out Irving.

"You have to look at the next guy," said Shumpert, who had been playing through a groin injury throughout the postseason. "You see one guy pushing through it, it gives you more inspiration to push. Like I've been telling everybody, I don't think anybody in the league at this point is healthy. I think everybody's got something going on, something's nagging them, but that desire to win outweighs whatever pain you're dealing with."

What some believed Shumpert insinuated was that Irving cared more about the possibility of a career-threatening injury than he did helping his team win a championship. But however real that likelihood, Irving did visit with famed surgeon Dr. James Andrews, who recommended that he stop treating his foot injury and focus on rehabilitating the knee. Andrews called for rest and Irving indeed sat out two games in a series that his team would have controlled with or without him. Though the Hawks had finished with the best record in the conference, they were no match for the Cavaliers despite the Big Three having been reduced to the Big One.

One could also claim, however, that the hustle and hard-nosed defense provided by the pest Dellavedova counteracted the loss of scoring due to Irving's absence. Cleveland had yet to lose when Irving played fewer than thirteen minutes (or not at all) in the playoffs. And that trend would continue in the title round. It could not be argued that Irving boasted far more talent than Dellavedova and that the latter provided superior defense, but it proved debatable that the team enjoyed better chemistry with Irving on the floor.

The ideal scenario was a healthy Irving on top of his game offensively and playing with intensity on the other side of the court. Dellavedova had become a cult figure in Cleveland with his passion and breakneck style, but he lost most of his offensive effectiveness when opponents began picking him up near midcourt. The defensive attention he suddenly warranted as a three-point threat and deft passer resulted in tighter coverage that he simply could not overcome because of his lack of quickness. And with Love sidelined for the finals, the Cavaliers needed Irving to take some of the scoring load off James. They otherwise could never match the firepower of Steph Curry, Klay Thompson, and the rest of the Warriors.

All seemed well when Irving returned to action to score 16 points in twenty-two minutes to help polish off the Hawks. The treatment prescribed by Dr. Andrews had given him confidence that his knee could survive the stop-and-go action required of point guards in the NBA, especially given the explosiveness of Irving, whose effectiveness was based on quick movement as a ball handler and rising enough on lay-ups and jumpers to prevent taller opponents (which included most everyone on the court) from blocking his shots.

That self-assurance shined through in Game 1 against Golden State.

The Cavaliers hung around throughout regulation as Irving and James scored or assisted on every basket in the fourth quarter. Irving even made a rare defensive stand, rising high to block a Curry shot from behind with thirty-eight seconds remaining and the score tied. And then . . . if only. If only James had buried the Warriors with his jumper with three seconds left. If only Shumpert had nailed his potential game-winner after tracking down the offensive rebound. If only *something* had happened to prevent overtime. Then disaster could not have struck.

Actually, a major catastrophe followed a minor one. The smaller catastrophe was a Cavalier collapse that resulted in a 10–0 Warrior overtime blitz that put the game away. Cleveland didn't even score in the extra session until James hit a driving lay-up with nine seconds left. By that time, the bigger calamity had seemingly killed any chance for a championship. That is when Irving's left knee collided with that of Klay Thompson as he tried to drive by the Golden State guard. Irving fell to the floor in agony and limped to the locker room, aided by trainer Steve Spiro. Irving, who had so diligently rehabbed and treated the knee with the express purpose of regaining his health for the finals, could not simply internalize his frustration and anger. He fired his jersey onto the concrete floor. And he knew this was no tweak. The pain level told him a very different story. So did the ice bag on his knee and his body language as he sat in front of his locker. A black towel draped over his head might have been hiding tears.

Dr. Parker maneuvered the knee in the training room. He detected no ligament damage. Irving spoke hopefully when addressing the media, but the crutches with which he left the arena told a dreary tale. He was soon diagnosed with a fractured kneecap that would require at least three or four months of recovery. The threat of even losing part of the following season became a reality. Irving sent out an Instagram message upon learning of his fate. It read:

> I want to thank everyone for the well wishes. Saddened by the way I had to go out, but it doesn't take away from being a part of a special playoff run with my brothers. Truly means a lot for all the support and

love. I gave it everything I had and have no regrets. I love this game no matter what and I'll be back soon. To my brothers: You already know what the deal is.

The deal was not only that James would be virtually forced to go solo in seeking to overcome the powerful Warriors. It was also that Blatt had played Irving a whopping forty-four minutes in the opener. That was quite a workload given that Irving had been sidelined for two full games against the Hawks and was still early in the recovery stage of the original knee injury. Drederick Irving spoke with general manager David Griffin. So did agent Jeff Wechsler, who looked stunned after visiting his client in the training room. Whether either or both were angry at Blatt for keeping Kyrie on the court for so long is only speculation. But the issue forced Blatt to explain his reasoning.

"There were no minute restrictions coming into Game 1," he said. "There were no minute restrictions in Game 4 against Atlanta. My take on the injury was that he got kneed in the side of his knee. It was a contact injury and the result was a fracture of the kneecap."

Reports surfaced that Drederick Irving and Wechsler had been urging the Cavaliers to remain cautious with Kyrie as the playoffs played out. Their concern was justifiable. After all, he was just twenty-three years old and many players have lost careers to injury, especially to the knee. But their concerns clashed with those of the Cavaliers, who in their forty-five years of existence had not won an NBA title and had only reached the finals once. The team had claimed that Irving's knee issue was merely tendinitis and players had even hinted when he missed two games against Atlanta that he should have been playing through it. They were questioning his guts and manhood.

As everyone simmered, the issue had already become water under the bridge. Nobody could challenge this injury and the Cavaliers were forced to use Dellavedova as the starting point guard. His cult status grew as he helped the team win the next two games with a slow-down attack, ferocious defense, and, of course, the all-around dominance of

James. But when Warriors coach Steve Kerr countered with a smaller and quicker lineup, the weaknesses of Dellavedova were exposed, and the Cavaliers were overwhelmed. Their lack of a scorer without Irving or Love to aid James and force Golden State to divert at least some defensive attention resulted in what eventually became apparent would be an inevitable series defeat.

The first tumultuous season for the reborn Cavaliers was over. Another would begin without Irving, whose next challenge would not be improving his moves to the basket or gaining a greater defensive presence. It would be quite simply working his way back onto the court as quickly as possible.

9 Spreading His Wings

It was July 25, 2015. Nearly two months had passed since the fractured left kneecap ended Irving's season and, for all intents and purposes, the championship hopes of his team. The surgery was a success. He had been cleared to put pressure on his leg. He was at Mentor High School in a far-east suburb of Cleveland along with 550 kids who had signed up for the Kyrie Irving Basketball ProCamp. He spoke about the recovery process. But he emphasized his desire to mentor at the Mentor school. He yearned to teach the students the fine points of ballhandling, just as his father had passed that talent down to him a generation earlier.

Irving had rehabbed much of that summer at Pinecrest Physical Therapy near the office of agent Jeff Wechsler in Miami. He altered his diet and monitored his sleep patterns in his desire to be in peak condition upon his return. He showed some of his progress at Mentor by walking from station to station and even wowing the campers with a display of his dribbling wizardry. He had proven true the words of general manager David Griffin, who had told the media that Irving was coming along quite well. Irving had only sported a brace for two weeks before beginning his workouts. But the knee injuries he suffered during the Eastern Conference playoffs and NBA Finals proved taxing physically, mentally, and emotionally. Irving spoke about those challenges months before the first ball was bounced in the 2015–16 season, as well as his desire to help the Cavaliers despite his incapacity.

"It sucks when you're actually injured but it's a test of your will and patience and just continuing to stay involved in the game the best you can," he said. "That's what I tried to do. Be there for my teammates as much as possible, see them as much as possible, see our coaching staff as much as possible, and stay in tune with everything that's going on."

What was also going on was fatherhood. Irving became a dad in late November, but the circumstances proved less than ideal. He announced the birth of daughter Azurie Elizabeth Irving on Facebook and Instagram, the latter showing him looking lovingly at the new addition in his arms. He wrote about having named the girl after his beloved departed mother Elizabeth. One problem, however, was that Irving had broken up with the mother of the baby, and he had filed legal documents requesting a paternity test to determine if he was indeed the father. He had broken up with 2010 Miss Texas Andrea Wilson long before the birth of the child. Wilson, who required thirty-five hours of labor to deliver, spoke about their relationship in an interview with TMZ Sports.

"Kyrie has had no participation," she said. "He is only seeking custody to look good for the press. I've paid for and handled everything on my own without ANY support from him. I have no connection with him nor do I seek any connection to him."

Irving, who stated that he began dating Wilson in 2013 but that they had since separated, strongly denied the accusation. He issued a statement through attorney Jim Mueller claiming that his goal in seeking a paternity test was to become involved in the child's life if his fatherhood was indeed proven.

What was also going on in late November was that Irving had still not returned to the lineup despite his apparent readiness. Blatt exercised extreme caution with his star point guard—and his team was winning without him. Critics again raised the nagging question regarding Irving's value to the Cavaliers. Would his lack of defensive intensity and apparent disinterest in tallying assists as well as points plague the team upon his return or would he gain a heretofore unseen maturity on the court and blossom in other phases of his game? The Cavaliers were 17-7 in mid-December without Irving. They had not managed a better start to the regular season since 2008.

Blatt remained vigilant about not straining Irving even after his big star returned to the court. Irving played fewer than thirty minutes in thirteen of his first eighteen games back. He struggled to find his rhythm, hitting more than half his shots in just three of those games, including back-to-back brilliant performances against Toronto and Washington that provided hope for a hot streak before he fell back into a slump.

That slump added fuel to the fire of Wizards rival point guard John Wall, who became incensed when Irving forged ahead of him in the All-Star fan balloting despite Irving having played only three games at the time. Wall called it a joke, then his organization turned it into one a week later by showing a video during a second-half timeout in which fans wearing Irving jerseys were asked which player had earned their All-Star selection. Of course, they all said Wall. The video did not slip by the Cavaliers, who watched it with interest. It was certainly taken to heart by Irving, who tore the Wizards apart with 10 points in the fourth quarter to finish with 32 in one of his finest performances of the season as his team notched its fifth consecutive victory in a streak that would reach eight.

Irving was obviously motivated by the video but had expressed no animosity toward Wall. He understood the logic behind the anger. "There were no ill-will emotions; there was no personal beef between John and me," he said. "I respect him as a player, as a point guard in this league, and as a great player in this league. So for him to say that, the All-Star becomes a popularity contest and what the fans want to see. So their respective opinions [are] based on that. For me, my respect for what I have for John goes way beyond the court, so there was no ill-will beef or anything like that, but he did make a valid point on me only playing two games and he was Eastern Conference Player of the Month, so that kind of goes without saying."

The reaction was typical Irving. He always treated players and coaches respectfully. His desire to maintain positive public relationships and not offend proved itself again a few years later when he did not criticize James directly in his demand to be traded from Cleveland despite the issues he had with him.

Those issues had certainly taken hold as 2015 turned into 2016 and the Cavaliers continued to steamroll through a soft schedule with sheer talent. They were playing without passion, particularly on the defensive end. Multiple media reports described their locker room as a morgue. The players were joylessly going through the motions. A dismantling on their home court by visiting Golden State in a highly anticipated rematch of the 2015 NBA Finals proved fatal to Blatt. Despite his team rebounding with wins over Brooklyn and the tough Los Angeles Clippers to raise its record to 30-11 at the midpoint of the regular season, he was fired, and Lue was promoted to head coach.

Though Irving, and more so James, had paid lip service to the performance of Blatt, they had far more respect for Lue, who, unlike his predecessor, had played in the NBA. Lue, who hired Mike Longabardi as an offensive assistant, yearned to make it clear that he had not pushed Blatt out the door and had indeed been surprised at his ouster. He spoke immediately about getting his players in better shape so they could handle the rigors of an eighty-two-game regular-season schedule, the potential for twenty-eight more in the playoffs, and sustain the necessary energy to maximize their efforts both offensively and defensively while pushing the ball up the floor.

The result of Lue's takeover proved critical, if not immediate. Such was certainly true of Irving, who remained inconsistent, but whose flashes of brilliance became more frequent and dominating. Lue did not push Irving to become more of a pass-first point guard. Rather, he urged him to be even more aggressive offensively to take advantage of his immense scoring talents. The words were music to his ears. Irving had never felt comfortable with any other mind-set. He embarked on an incredible scoring binge when his knee had been deemed ready to carry him through thirty-five to forty minutes per game. He averaged nearly 25 points on 51 percent shooting during that stretch. Irving proved especially deadly with his crossover dribble and drives to the basket. His scoring explosion was achieved despite significant struggles from beyond the three-point arc.

Yet one still wondered to what extent his defensive liabilities negatively affected the team. A strange incident in Oklahoma in late February the night before an afternoon game against the powerful Thunder led to a team performance that provided fodder for such questions. Irving awoke in his hotel room at 3 a.m. itchy. Turning on the light revealed five huge bedbugs crawling about the sheets and pillow. He tried to sleep on the couch but wound up exhausted. He felt so sick the next day that he was taken to the locker room in the first quarter and never returned to action. Without him, the Cavaliers managed one of their best defensive efforts of the season. Trailing by 3 points upon his departure, they held the explosive Thunder, featuring Kevin Durant and Russell Westbrook, to 92 points on just 41 percent shooting in a blowout victory. Irving then returned to score 30 the next night, but the Cavaliers lost to mediocre Detroit. Though many factors weighed into that dichotomy, the lack of parallels between the levels of Irving's offensive performances and the overall effectiveness of his team proved puzzling nonetheless.

Irving continued to post big numbers. He averaged 23.4 points and 6 assists during one seven-game stretch in late February and early March. One of his proudest efforts was achieved against Kobe Bryant and the visiting Lakers. Irving yearned to shine in his last game against his retiring hero, the man with ailing knees and shoulder, who was a mere shadow of his former self. Irving had established a rare friendship with Bryant, who owned a reputation as being rather aloof with his basketball-playing comrades. The battle of the NBA stars was lopsided as Irving scored 35 points to 17 for the Lakers' legend. The two exchanged compliments.

"His mental approach and pursuit of perfection," Irving responded when asked what he learned from Bryant over the years. "Just watching him a ton. A ton. Not only him but a lot of guys that have come before me and have left a lasting legacy on this game. That's who you want to emulate as a young player. . . . For me I just know that it happens in steps and a lot of dedication. Being resilient and having a mental toughness separates you from the rest of the group. So I want to have that and [Bryant] is definitely one of those guys that I look to for advice and communicate with." Bryant too was effusive in his praise. "He has a killer mentality," said the sure-fire Hall of Famer about Irving. "He can shoot the long ball. His midrange game is excellent. And he can finish at the rim. He has all the tools there. The way he played tonight he can do this pretty much every night."

Bryant expressed an unusual opinion about team chemistry that he related to the Cavaliers. And it didn't include everyone chanting kumbaya and joining each other in a happy dance. "You have to have that inner conflict," he said. "You have to have that person that's really driving these things. From the Cavs' perspective, it's hard for me to tell from afar who should be that person. LeBron is not that person. LeBron, he brings people together. That's what he does naturally. He's phenomenal at it. But you have to have somebody else who's going to create that tension. Maybe it's Kyrie."

The notion that a player fomenting any level of anxiety among teammates can be a positive, let alone necessary for success, seemed a bit far-fetched. The Cavaliers were not the Oakland Athletics or New York Yankees of the 1970s. Irving was quick to agree with Bryant but mentioned nothing about creating tension. His interpretation of Bryant's statement was that every team needed a player who would hold teammates accountable, and he stated furthermore that he could embrace that role. "It's in my personality, I would agree with that," he said. "I think that in order for our team to be where we want to go, I have to step up and be that leader on our team other than LeBron. So I would agree with that. It's definitely in my personality. It's taken me a few years to kind of grow into that and kind of earn my teammates' respect and also hold myself accountable when I'm out there."

And that takes a level of maturity Irving admitted he did not always have since joining the Cavaliers four years earlier; on the verge of his twenty-fourth birthday and with expectations of himself and the team at its peak, he realized the need for growth mentally and emotionally. "I have to grow up quick, especially with this team," he said. "In order for us to be successful, I have to be a lot older than what my years show. So, it's been a learning experience since Day 1 that Bron has come back and being a championship-caliber team, I've had to grow up quick. It hasn't been perfect. I've made a lot of mistakes along the way, but one thing I can bank on is when I get it, I get it, and we get rolling. That's the way it should be. It's taken time but I'm definitely assuming that role of being one of the guys that [has] the other voice, other than LeBron and [Tyronn Lue]."

There was one problem. Irving had still not accomplished that level of consistency overall, nor an intensity on defense, to be an ideal example for teammates to follow. He suffered through quite the opposite in an effort against young, talented Raptors point guard Kyle Lowry, who schooled him for 43 points, including the game-winning shot at the buzzer. Irving had won previous competitions in the budding rivalry, but on this night, he scored just 10 points on 4-of-16 shooting and managed a mere 1 assist. That Lowry had beaten out Irving for an All-Star Game berth (Irving had been voted in twice before and in the end was indeed overlooked due to losing much of the early season to injury) made the dominance particularly troubling.

Far more troubling were reports of dissension in the ranks, particularly between Irving and James. That was not what Bryant had in mind when he spoke about creating tension. One cannot be certain when the seeds of Irving's discontent had been planted since the return of James to Cleveland—perhaps from the beginning. But on this occasion, Irving hinted at a problem by not denying there was one. He stated after the host Cavaliers required a late rally against Indiana to avoid a third straight defeat that misunderstanding between players was a natural occurrence on sports teams. Time was running out on the regular season. March was fast approaching, and the Cavaliers were playing their worst ball since Irving returned from the knee injury. Rather than hitting their stride to peak for the playoffs, they were breaking apart.

James continued to play the role of big brother to Irving. It was in his DNA to be a teacher, to want to use his experience and one of the highest basketball IQs in NBA history to raise the level of hoops consciousness in others. But many believed that Irving flatly rejected the notion that he needed James to teach him anything about playing the sport. Irving wanted to be placed on the same pedestal as his teammate. He eventually concluded that was impossible. It was that realization that motivated Irving to demand a trade after the 2016–17 season.

He was not at that point yet. But the media spotlight given to James bothered Irving well before that. "What I did notice in the locker room, where there were two stalls between him and LeBron, was that he wanted to be center stage," offered *News-Herald* beat writer Jeff Schudel. "I think it bothered Kyrie that he was not the focus of everyone's attention. Sometimes LeBron would needle him a little but subtly and Kyrie would get irritated by that. When we talked to those guys in the playoffs, particularly at the press table, 80 percent of the questions would be directed at LeBron. Kyrie could have a great game and it would always be LeBron this, LeBron that, or 'LeBron, what did you think of Kyrie?' I think that did get under his skin a little bit."

Things got worse before they got better for Irving. A personal tragedy threatened to take his heart and mind out of focus. He had been dating singer Kehlani Parrish throughout the season. But she broke off the relationship in March to renew one with fellow recording artist Jahron Brathwaite, more commonly known as PartyNextDoor. The media picked up on the story and accused Parrish of cheating on Irving. The negative national attention played a role in Parrish attempting suicide late that month.

Making matters more uncomfortable was that Parrish was a Warriors fan who had recorded a song the previous summer celebrating her favorite team's NBA Finals triumph over Cleveland. It seemed the entire world was caving in on Irving. Fate even added an illness that caused him to miss time. His game fell apart throughout that period. He made just 33 of 104 shots during a six-game stretch that included efforts of 6-for-22 and 5-for-23 from the field.

The disturbing events forced a man who generally yearned to keep his private life private to address the situation. Irving sought to minimize the damage by speaking about far more serious hardships. After all, this was a young man who lost his mother at age four. "It hasn't been difficult," he said. "I've been through a ton of adversity in my life. There's nothing anything or anyone can say that I can't get through. I've been through enough already in my short twenty-four years that most people can say for their entire lives."

Another issue had reared its ugly head in mid-March when Irving recorded just one assist in a taut defeat of Dallas. At one point in the second quarter he aimlessly dribbled out the 24-second clock seeking an opening never created and finally hoisted up a missed jumper as his teammates stood around. With James resting that night, the aggressiveness encouraged by Lue had been taken to a degree that frustrated and angered his teammates. Pride as NBA players can be wounded when ignored and seemingly mistrusted on the court. A deeper examination of the game revealed that Irving led the team in passes, including eight that would have resulted in assists had shots been made. But though Irving clinched the win with a steal and scored 33 points, he required a season-high 28 shots to reach that total and was amid a ten-game stretch in which he averaged just 4.3 assists and managed more than 5 only once. Meanwhile, his teammates couldn't wait until James and his pass-first mentality returned.

If Irving remained affected by any professional and personal demons when the playoffs rolled around, it didn't show. He and his teammates raised their intensity to a level far greater than what was seen at any point in the regular season. Such had been a trademark of James-led teams since he left for Miami, while the competitive juices flowed stronger for Irving as well. That was a necessity—one knew that any opponent of the defending Eastern Conference champions was destined to be firing on all emotional cylinders.

Despite any issues bubbling beneath the surface, the Cavaliers were also fired up for the playoffs, as well as confident. Irving raised many an eyebrow when he declared Cleveland the team to beat despite the absurd, record-breaking 73-9 mark compiled by Golden State. Veteran players such as well-liked Channing Frye worked to bring emotional cohesion to the group. The Cavaliers clinched home-court advantage throughout the Eastern Conference playoffs, Irving had fully recovered from knee surgery and had worked himself into fine shape, and a comparatively weak conference appeared to provide little competition for such a talented bunch. A historic run was about to begin.

10 The Run and "The Shot"

Tyronn Lue had a special place in his heart and memory for Kyrie Irving. The Cleveland coach recalled with some bitterness how his role was altered in the NBA after a stellar college career at the University of Nebraska. He too thrived as a scoring point guard with the Cornhuskers, averaging 21.2 points as a junior before jumping to the pros. He had hoisted 17 shots per game in college, but never matched that total in any NBA game until his sixth season, the first in which he averaged more than 10 points per game. Lue parlayed his talents into an eleven-year pro career, but never served as a full-time starter and only took 10 shots or more per game in one season.

The Cavaliers' coach understood that Irving boasted far more talent and did not want him to be saddled with a role that failed to suit his strengths. "Jason Kidd, [Rajon] Rondo, that's not who Kyrie is," Lue said. "That's not going to happen. Kyrie's passing ability comes off his aggressiveness. If he looks to pass [first], that takes away his aggressiveness, and that's not who he is. [When] he's aggressive, looking to score, that opens up his passing, a lot like I was in college."

It could be argued that nothing opened up Irving's willingness to pass and that Lue was only correct in theory. But it was that mind-set—as well as a full-court, fast-break style that would prevent defenses from getting set and allow shooters such as Love and J. R. Smith to find space while creating opportunities for driving lay-ups—that Lue stressed to Irving heading into the 2016 playoffs.

The first barrier to Cleveland's first major sports championship in fifty-two years was the Detroit Pistons. Determined to play a physical style inside, the Pistons dared Irving and James to score from the perimeter. Both had struggled to hit three-pointers in the first half of the season, but Irving in particular sizzled from deep thereafter, shooting 42 percent from beyond the arc. He maintained that torrid pace and then some against the Pistons, nailing 16 of 34 (47 percent). His half-court heave at Detroit to break a tie heading into the fourth quarter of Game 4 began to push the final dagger into the hearts of the Pistons and their fans in completing the sweep. Irving paced both teams with an average of 27.5 points per game, marking only the second time in thirty-four playoff series of James' remarkable career that he did not lead his team in scoring.

So heated was this battle and so physical were the desperate Pistons that they resorted to roughhousing. Defensive-oriented center Andre Drummond elbowed James in the neck, leading James to complain when Drummond was not suspended by the NBA and charge the league with being more likely to allow dirty hits against him.

After breaking a tie with the midcourt shot at the third-quarter buzzer in Game 4, Irving proved his defensive potential with seconds remaining and the Cavaliers clutching a 100–98 lead. He furiously guarded Pistons explosive guard Reggie Jackson on a full-court drive to the basket, forcing him to take an off-balance heave that barely grazed the rim. Irving's defense, which had been greatly and rightfully criticized since he entered the league, had risen to the occasion when needed the most. And when it was over, as he was being hugged by teammates, he shouted "bye-bye" to fans who had heckled him throughout. His face was filled with vengeful joy.

Irving and the Cavaliers embraced their momentum and ran with it into the Eastern Conference semifinals against Atlanta. They simply bombed the Hawks into oblivion with 77 three-pointers. Irving hit an amazing 67 percent of his attempts from beyond the arc in the four-game sweep. He displayed his entire arsenal, preventing Atlanta from keying on any piece of his offensive weaponry. He attacked the basket relentlessly and even belied his reputation as a score-first point guard at times by passing the ball off to open shooters. He averaged 6.5 assists in the series as James and long-range marksmen Love and Smith had a field day taking his feeds and draining threes.

The conference finals against Toronto brought new challenges for Irving and a personal rematch against Kyle Lowry. Despite an awful Game 3 in which Irving missed 16 of 19 shots, it was no contest. Irving outshot Lowry, finished with more points, steals, and assists, and even had a better defensive rating. The Cavaliers won their three home games by an average of 29 points and polished off the Raptors with a 113–87 trouncing in Toronto as Irving tallied 30 points and a game-high 9 assists. His team was destined for an NBA Finals rematch against Golden State. And this time around—unlike the year before—they would come to battle with a healthy Irving and Love.

The series promised another one-on-one spotlight clash for Irving, this time against two-time NBA Most Valuable Player Stephen Curry. The league was top-heavy with premier point guards, but Curry had earned the distinction as the best of the best. His shooting range was seemingly unlimited, and he boasted enough talent and willingness as a passer and defender to be considered a complete player. That versatility is where critics of Irving drew the line between the two stars. Nobody doubted Irving's pure offensive brilliance. But most doubted his ability to outplay Curry on the biggest stage.

Some even felt that trying to keep up with Curry on the defensive end would diminish Irving's offensive effectiveness. But in the 2016 NBA Finals, with the hopes and dreams of millions of Cleveland fans who had not experienced the joy of a major sports championship since the Browns upset the Colts for the NFL crown in 1964, it turned out to be the other way around. It was Curry whose offense suffered, his energy sapped by fruitlessly working to hang against Irving's stop-and-go and crossover dribbling to the hoop and bombs from deep. Irving had simply outplayed Lowry a round earlier. He destroyed Curry for all the marbles.

It did not start out that way. Irving hit just 12 of 36 shots as the Cavaliers were clobbered in Games 1 and 2 at Golden State. The Warriors utilized a defensive strategy on pick-and-rolls against him that worked to successfully shut him down in isolation and prevent him from attacking the basket. The result was indecision and dribbling the ball without moving it as seconds dripped off the shot clock. He was held without an assist until the fourth quarter of Game 2, an embarrassing 33-point defeat that had even some basketball experts anticipating a sweep.

Irving was accused of allowing his offensive struggles to take away from his defensive intensity. He was burned repeatedly on drives to the hoop. His problems seemed to have justified the research of the Harvard College Sports Analysis Collective, a think tank consisting of the prestigious university students, who concluded that Irving should be benched. Their rationale was that his usual offensive brilliance did not tip a positive balance against his selfishness with the ball and poor defense.

The analysis, which was posted just before the finals, cited that Irving ranked a woeful eighty-third among eighty-five qualifying point guards during the regular season in defensive real plus-minus, which measures the average net point differential of a player over 100 defensive possessions. The Harvard Collective then went on to make the following comparisons between Irving and backup Matthew Dellavedova both offensively and defensively in its claim that Irving should be removed from the starting lineup:

> If we zero in even further on the Kyrie vs. [Dellavedova] debate with a little help from our friends at NBAwowy, we find that in the 102 postseason minutes that LeBron and Delly have been on the court with Kyrie on the bench, opponents are scoring just 0.788 points per possession and shooting just 32 percent from three-point range, compared to 1.02 points per possession and 34.6 percent from three with Delly off and Kyrie on. These statistics are perhaps skewed by Kyrie playing against

starters and Delly playing against benches, but that almost certainly does not account for such a dramatic difference. Dellavedova has always been a better defender than Kyrie, and has continued to be better in the Playoffs, and will undoubtedly be better at slowing down Steph Curry.

The question remains, then, is Kyrie's offense good enough to make none of this matter? He's averaging 24 points and 5 assists in the Playoffs—surely you don't just bench a guy like that? For all his impressive drives and 25-plus point games, however, Kyrie isn't moving the needle much on offense for the Cavs. When LeBron and Kyrie have shared the court this postseason, Cleveland has scored 1.14 points per possession when Kyrie goes off, they score 1.13. Additionally, it is realistic to expect the Cavs to move to a more LeBron-centric offense against and increase his 28 percent usage rate to something closer to the 40 percent usage rate he had in last year's Finals, which he nearly won by himself. Should that happen, the fact that Dellavedova shot 46 percent on catch-and-shoot threes this year and Kyrie shot just 35 percent is another nail in Irving's coffin.

Some believed there were more holes in that theory than in Irving's defensive game. Benching Irving, which of course was never considered by Lue, would have allowed the Warriors to place far greater defensive focus on James and Love. After all, one reason Dellavedova hit nearly 50 percent beyond the arc is that he received such little attention that he found himself open. Another flaw in the thinking was that Dellavedova and his breakneck style was unsuited to remain effective for thirty to thirty-five minutes per game. He had become so bushed when forced into the starting lineup during the 2015 finals that he was hospitalized for dehydration.

Though most considered the paper overanalytical and absurd, it did reflect the thinking of many who were frustrated by the good, bad, and ugly of Irving's game. James even indicated without mentioning Irving's name that those who were not willing to follow the game plan could find themselves unceremoniously banished to the sideline by Lue.

Lue had another idea. He would reason with Irving. But rather than beg him to pass the ball more or work harder defensively, he simply reinforced in him the need to be his aggressive and confident self. He told him to shoot the ball or drive quickly rather than allow the defense to get settled. Lue conceded to Irving that nobody could completely shut down Curry. But the coach sought to buoy his confidence by reminding him that he too was unstoppable.

Irving had earned a reputation, particularly since the return of James, as a clutch performer. He had not yet had an opportunity to rise to the occasion on the biggest stage of the basketball world—the NBA Finals. But he was about to. Irving became arguably the best player on the court for the rest of the series—and that included the immortal James. He tallied 30 points and 8 assists in a rout of the Warriors in Game 3 and added 34 in a defeat two nights later that placed the Cavaliers on the precipice of elimination.

That is when Irving raised his level of play from brilliant to otherworldly. The series returned to Golden State for Game 5. Champagne had been placed in the Warriors locker room in anticipation of a celebration. The loss of defensive-oriented power forward Draymond Green to a suspension for a dirty hit on James dampened their fans' hopes a bit, but the dominance of a team that set an NBA record by winning seventy-three games in the regular season had many of them assuming it was over.

Irving had other ideas. He turned Curry inside out. His stop-and-go dribbling and ability to score off of drives and pull-up jumpers had Curry guessing, slipping, and sliding. Irving was hitting from all of the court, including beyond the three-point line. He transformed a tie into a Cleveland blowout in a second half of the greatest game of his career to date, given the enormity of the battle. He scored on a driving lay-up to give the Cavaliers a lead they would never relinquish. He nailed a three-pointer, then another two minutes later. The fourth quarter could have been titled The Kyrie Irving Show. He scored 10 consecutive Cleveland points during one stretch on moves that astounded the awe-struck fans in Oakland and millions more watching around the world. And when the last basketball had been bounced, he had finished with 41 points on an amazing 17-of-24 shooting spree while holding Curry to 25 on a chilly 8-for-25 from the field.

James added 41 to mark the first time in NBA history that teammates scored 40 points or more in one NBA Finals game. But James preferred to praise his teammate rather than the man he saw in the mirror. It was acclamation of the highest order considering the source. "It's probably one of the greatest performances I've ever seen live," James said of Irving's effort.

Such heroics were hardly required when the series returned to Cleveland for Game 6. The Cavaliers performed with far more energy than the lifeless and dispirited Warriors, blowing them out from the start as James again scored 41 in a 115–101 triumph that forced a deciding game in Oakland. So frustrated was the foul-plagued Curry that he exploded against the officials in the fourth quarter and got tossed from the game.

That Irving was performing better defensively in the finals is undeniable. But he only ranked in the middle of all participants in defensive metrics over the last seven games of the playoffs, which covered the series against Golden State. It can be argued that Curry's offensive wounds were more self-inflicted than caused by Irving. The NBA Most Valuable Player shot just 40 percent from the field and averaged more than 4 turnovers a game. He saved his worst for last in Game 7.

The two offensive juggernauts would embark on a titanic defensive struggle with the title on the line. Neither team could find its rhythm or shooting touch. Another Irving explosion in the third quarter in which he again scored 10 straight points gave his team a 68–61 lead, but the Cavaliers could not sustain it. Golden State forged ahead by 1 point heading into the fourth quarter and a tense seesaw battle emerged. A basket by Warriors sharpshooter Klay Thompson tied it at 89–89 with 4:39 left. There the score remained for nearly the next four minutes. The teams combined to miss the next 12 shots. Included was an awkward runner by Irving that missed badly.

The Cavaliers were in a battle of wills. Less than a minute remained in a clash for the crown. It seemed that the score had been tied at 89 interminably. Irving appreciated all that hung in the balance. His team had not won a championship since its inception in 1970. Not since 1964 had the city derided for decades as the "Mistake by the Lake" celebrated with a parade down Euclid Avenue. The fervent hopes of millions rested upon his shoulders. Irving did not merely accept the pressure. He embraced it. It was *his* time now.

James graced the same court, but the superstar had suggested to Lue that the next play be designed for Irving. The mantle of assassin had been passed. Irving had earned the reputation as the deadliest one-on-one player in basketball. And he was about to prove himself worthy of it.

Kyrie Irving had that look in his eyes, proclaiming himself on an unstoppable mission. It was a glare that could burn a hole in the hardwood and strike fear in the hearts and minds of defenders.

Soon he was going solo against Curry. As colorful TV commentator Mark Jackson described the moment: "It was time to dance." And Irving was going to lead. The game clock ticked down to 55 seconds. Curry could not play Irving too closely for fear that the ballhandling wizard would drive past him to the basket. Irving dribbled inches behind the three-point arc. He bounced the ball through his legs, soared straight up, and launched beyond the fingertips of Curry's outstretched hand.

Swish!

The biggest shot in Cavaliers history, and perhaps the most epic ever witnessed, fell with feathery smoothness through the net. Irving played the rest of the game like a man possessed. After feisty Love defense forced a Curry miss, network analyst Jeff Van Gundy famously stressed to his TV audience that the Cavaliers needed to eat precious seconds off the clock. But Irving still had that look in his eye. His killer instinct drove him to the basket. He nearly dribbled the ball out of bounds but managed to find a free Love in the frontcourt. His overzealousness could have proven disastrous.

"He was never asked to my knowledge what the hell he was doing on that play," said *Cleveland Plain Dealer* columnist Bill Livingston. "That could have been one of the greatest Cavalier gooferoos ever. Then he went too soon at the end of the game too."

It seemed at the moment of reckoning that Irving could play no other way. After a Golden State foul stopped the clock, he *again* dispensed with common sense and headed to the hoop. This time he found James barreling to the basket for a pass that resulted in a foul shot that clinched victory.

Irving had played the role of hero in an epic triumph—it marked the first time any NBA team had rebounded from a 3–1 deficit to win in the finals. What was soon simply pronounced as "The Shot" was deemed by the *Wall Street Journal* as the biggest heave in NBA history. Irving, who admitted he had barely slept over the 48 hours before the game, spoke about how his emotional connection to Bryant helped him overcome the pressure of the moment. Irving too became "The Black Mamba" by channeling his inner Kobe. He had remained in that mode after telling his teammates around the end of the first half that he needed to settle in after a slow start. "That moment right there happened, and I was like, 'Okay, I'm fine,'" Irving said. "And all I was thinking about in the back of my mind was mamba mentality. Just mamba mentality, that's all I was thinking."

Irving also spoke lovingly about his teammates, with whom his rocky journey had ended, at least at that point, with respect and admiration. "I'm just really thankful to be a part of history like this and it to be done with the group that I have in that locker room, thus making history and etching our names forever in NBA history," he said.

The team that made history motivated more than a million delirious fans to converge on downtown Cleveland for a parade that brought joy to their hearts and pride to a once-beleaguered city. Irving and his teammates embraced the moment. They spoke individually to the masses, yet they spoke as one. Irving had played such a significant role in the achievement that some claimed that he—not James—should have been named NBA Finals Most Valuable Player. Irving took a backseat to no one. The statistical differences between he and James in minutes played, shots taken, and points scored were negligible. Irving had reached superstar status. One assumed he had grown perfectly content playing alongside James on an NBA champion.

One assumed wrong. The driving force of Kyrie Irving that made him one of the most enigmatic figures in American sports would soon be picking up speed.

11 The Off-Season of Dreams

Two days had passed since The Good Shot had replaced The Bad Shot in the hearts and minds of Cleveland fans forever. The Good Shot was the three-pointer that Kyrie Irving nailed to give the city its first championship in more than half a century. The Bad Shot was one of many symbols of heartache (including The Drive, The Fumble, and The Mesa Meltdown) that had burdened northeast Ohio for years—including the legendary Michael Jordan buzzer-beating Game 5 jumper that turned a dream into a nightmare in the first round of the 1989 Eastern Conference playoffs.

Irving relished the moment as he joined his father, sister, and close friends at the dining room table the day before the biggest parade in Cleveland history. Suddenly he became solemn, nearly tearful, as he glimpsed at the spot where the mother he lost at age four would have sat. He had barely gotten to know her, but he understood the impact she had made on his life and the lives of those family members who meant so much to him. "I just really want to thank everyone for their support," he said.

The message was the same to teammates when Irving was provided the opportunity to speak to them in front of an estimated 1.2 million fans who streamed into downtown Cleveland to celebrate. "We're all together and bonded for life and this is an unbelievable ride that I'll remember for the rest of my life," he said. "The only question that can be ever be said about this team is, what's next? So, from the bottom of my heart, this is a very special year. I wouldn't trade it for the world. I love y'all."

Irving preceded that verbal love letter by revealing that he had watched The Block on replay more than his own dagger shot. The former was the incredible run-down swat of an Andre Iguodala lay-up by James that would have given Golden State a 91–89 lead with a couple of minutes remaining. After all, Irving stated, The Shot would not have been possible without The Block. Such was not necessarily true, as Irving's three-pointer would have still given Cleveland the lead, though it would have altered the strategy for the Warriors on their next possession. But Irving painted a bigger picture when he expressed his appreciation for James and his teammates and indicated a curiosity about what the Cavaliers could achieve in the near future. That future included a demanded departure that many believe he would have insisted upon immediately had the timing been right. One does not ask to be traded after winning a championship.

One does, however, drop hints. Irving did so during the finals, when he talked about fading from the spotlight upon the arrival of James. "Having just a tremendously great player like that come to your team, and you see yourself being one of those great players eventually, and then he ends up joining it, and then now you have to almost take a step back and observe," Irving said. "Finding that balance is one of the toughest things to do because you have so much belief and confidence in yourself. . . . Selfishly, I always wanted to just show everyone in the whole entire world exactly what I was every single time."

Critics of what they believed to be twisted logic argued that Irving did show the entire world what he was during the finals and more so since James arrived than previously. What Irving showed when he was indeed the featured attraction was that he could not transform the Cavaliers into a contender, that he proved himself either untrusting of his teammates on the offensive end or unwilling to fully involve them, that he lacked the desire to play as hard on defense as he did at the other end of the court.

Of course, he displayed the same shortcomings after he was joined by James. But he did work tirelessly to mesh with The King, to find that balance about which he spoke. Some believe that he benefited greatly from it. They argue that the defensive attention required against James provided him greater freedom to display his ballhandling wizardry in isolation.

The on-court relationship they achieved reached a pinnacle in the finals. It placed a last nail in the Warriors' coffin at the end of Game 7 when Irving bolted to the hoop and found a cutting James for what would have been a title-clinching dunk but wound up as a title-clinching foul shot. One can disparage Irving for his desire to play second banana to no one, but not for any unwillingness to work with James. That is the view of *Medina Gazette* beat writer Noland, who rejects the notion that James made Irving a better player.

"I don't think he got nearly enough credit for his ability to thrive and prosper and improve while playing with James," Noland said. "He did it as well as any LeBron James teammate ever has and never lost his ability to play the game individually. He never lost his confidence, and to his credit never complained publicly about not getting even more opportunities. He maximized the ones he got and there were games he would score 12 points in three minutes when he really caught fire. One of the misnomers with LeBron is that he makes everybody better and I think that's 100 percent true when it comes to the Mike Millers or Kyle Korvers or James Joneses of the world—specialists who need help to be better. When you look back at LeBron James's career he doesn't make other star players better necessarily, which we saw with Kevin Love. But Kyrie's numbers went up and I think they went up because of Kyrie, not because of LeBron James.

"LeBron is the ultimate alpha dog. He never ever had to play where he wasn't not only the best player on his team but one of the best players period. That goes back to high school and AAU. . . . In a perfect world LeBron wanted to take [Irving] under his wing and impart all his knowledge on him, not just on the court but off. Like how to be a success businesswise and how to get the media on your side rather than against you, how to rise up in big games, how to prepare, how to eat, how to train. He was willing to share with Kyrie about all those things. But Kyrie is a supremely confident individual who was like, I can figure those things out on my own, I don't need a big brother. Kyrie didn't want to be the student, he wanted to be the guy. And he felt that as long as he was on the same team with LeBron he was never going to have the opportunity to fully go out and show how good he could be and how good he could make the team be."

Those who argued that Irving did not trust his teammates to finish what he started on the floor gained verbal ammunition during the 2016 Summer Olympics in Rio. Sharing the court with nothing but superstars (though James wasn't one of them), he compiled numbers far more associated with traditional point guards as the United States captured its third consecutive gold medal. Irving averaged 11.4 points in twenty-two minutes per game to place third on the team behind Kevin Durant and Carmelo Anthony. But he easily led the Americans with an average of 4.9 assists. His assists-per-minute ratio in the Olympics far exceeded that of any of his NBA seasons.

Cleveland fans criticized Irving when he stated before the Olympics that the achievements of earning gold and winning the NBA title were "pretty much the same." The complaints were coming from a fan base that had not tasted such joy in fifty-two years. And Irving did stretch the bounds of reality when he compared the two. Team USA from 1936 to 2016 won fifteen of eighteen gold medals and owned a record of 138-5. Winning the Olympics, particularly with a roster of NBA all-stars, is expected. The Cavaliers tipped off their existence in 1970 and had never snagged a crown until 2016. They were decided underdogs against the Warriors. Irving, however, did not back off his claim. He doubled down, making no attempt to placate Cleveland fans or elevate the NBA crown to a higher standing.

"What's great about that is that it's . . . my opinion," Irving said. "Meaning that I personally feel that way. It doesn't matter what anyone else thinks about it. I do know that the journeys are different between getting a gold medal and winning an NBA championship. The competition is different. There are a lot of things that factor. In terms of the feeling and the accomplishment, in my opinion, for me, they're almost the same. Because neither one is guaranteed. There's no guarantee that we're gonna win a gold medal. There's no guarantee going into the season that you're going to win an NBA championship."

The Summer Games forced Irving to pass on a promise he'd made to his father. After Irving left Duke following his eleven-game season in 2011 he made a pact with Pop that he would earn his degree within five years. He told reporters at the NBA Combine and the *Duke Chronicle* that year that the plan to earn his diploma had begun to be formulated with a major in sociology or psychology. But his commitment to USA Basketball in 2012, 2014, and 2016, as well as the limited number of online courses the school offers, combined to ruin those plans. And though some Duke alumni who left early to play in the NBA attended summer classes to complete their college educations, Irving was not among them. "[I want] to do what I can in the league, make sure I leave a legacy in the NBA, and then when I leave the game of basketball, then I'll focus on the next step of my life," he said.

Whether that meant returning to school could only be speculated. Irving was evolving. He was branching out professionally and intellectually while taking stronger social and political stands. He had since joining the NBA embraced opportunities to show he cared about those less fortunate. Irving joined former basketball star Dikembe Mutombo in 2013 on a trip to South Africa for the UNICEF Schools for Africa initiative. He visited schools in Soweto and Randfontein and spoke with students at institutions with high drop-out rates about the importance of completing their educations. He led kids in physical education programs and a basketball clinic, as well as an art project. And he came away with an appreciation of the determination of the children in the face of poverty and in a society still ravaged by the vestiges of apartheid. "Even with the challenges they face, it was inspiring to see how much the kids want to learn and how hard the teachers are working," he said. "I saw firsthand how early childhood education and school sports activities are making a difference in these kids' lives."

Irving also showed signs of political consciousness and conviction in

2014 when he donned an "I Can't Breathe" warm-up shirt before a game in 2014 to place a spotlight on the death of African American Eric Garner, who had uttered those words while being roughly handled by New York police officers. And in late 2016 Irving would become aware of Sioux protests in South Dakota against the proposed Keystone XL pipeline, to which he tweeted his support. He also gained a greater appreciation of his mother's ties to the Standing Rock Indian Reservation before her adoption. Elizabeth had later experienced racism growing up in the predominantly white Puyallup suburb of Tacoma, Washington, as a girl of mixed descent, having been called "nigger" by some classmates as she walked home from school. Many offspring who lose parents around the age of four and whose memories of them are either faint or nonexistent never develop a desire to learn about their lives or strengthen their emotional ties to them. Such was not true of Irving. He declared himself a Sioux a few months after expressing his solidarity with the Native Americans and two years before his highly publicized visit to Standing Rock during which he was given the name Little Mountain in a formal ceremony.

Little Mountain had scaled a big mountain. He had helped the Cavaliers win an NBA championship and outperformed the league's Most Valuable Player in the process. But one could not blame him for feeling slighted. He received little consideration for a finals MVP that James won without a second thought. And in five seasons he had yet to earn first- or second-team All-NBA honors, landing on the third team only in 2015 before James had returned to Cleveland. That he was being overshadowed by The King was a given. But that he was truly deserving of greater consideration for postseason honors could certainly be disputed. Irving had yet to expand his overall game as a facilitator, distributor, or defender. Those who finished ahead of him, including Chris Paul, Russell Westbrook, and Stephen Curry, could not only score with the best of them, but dished out far more assists. Neither Russell nor Curry in particular fell into the category of traditional point guard. But they proved nightly that one could fill up the hoop and help others do the same.

Irving had proven himself the most talented ball handler and finisher in the sport. His fearlessness and ability to rise to any challenge with games, and even championships, on the line could not be questioned. But his overall numbers paled in comparison to those of the premier point guards in the NBA. It remained to be seen if he could elevate his all-around play and production sharing the court with James as the 2016–17 season approached. Or if he even wanted to share the court with James.

1. Irving takes a break in the 2008–9 season, during a stellar high school career that landed him a full ride at Duke University. Bryan Horowitz / https://creativecommons.org/licenses/by-sa/2.0/.

2. Future NBA standout Michael Kidd-Gilchrist (front) and Irving combined to make a potent dynamic duo at St. Patrick's during the 2008–9 season. Bryan Horowitz / https://creativecommons.org/licenses/by-sa/2.0/.

3. Irving (left) and future NBA rival Harrison Barnes listen to coaching instructions during the 2010 Nike Hoops Summit in Portland, Oregon. Wikimedia Commons / https://creativecommons.org/licenses/by-sa/3.0/deed.en.

4. Showing his hops, Irving leaps to score in front of a home crowd at Duke in November 2010. Jon Gardiner/Duke Photography.

5. Irving directs traffic during his college debut against Princeton in November 2010. He'd finish the game with 17 points and 9 assists. Jon Gardiner/Duke Photography.

6. Irving displays that quick first step in taking a Colgate defender to the basket during an early-season victory in 2010. Jon Gardiner/Duke Photography.

7. Two smiling faces—Irving poses with a fan during his Duke days in October 2010. Bryan Horowitz / https://creativecommons.org/licenses/by-sa/2.0/.

8. Was Irving better than Wizards star point guard John Wall or vice versa? The argument had begun by the time this photo was taken in April 2012. Erik Drost / https://creativecommons.org/licenses/by/2.0/.

9. An animated Irving looks downcourt during a 2013 exhibition game before his third NBA season with the Cavaliers. Erik Drost / https://creativecommons.org/licenses/by/2.0/.

10. Irving hooks one over almost-Cavalier Andrew Wiggins during a 29-point performance in a Cleveland victory against Minnesota two days before Christmas in 2014. Erik Drost / https://creativecommons.org/licenses/by/2.0/deed.en.

11. Premier Oklahoma City point guard Russell Westbrook zeroes in on a focused Irving during a sixth straight victory in a Cavalier winning streak that would reach 12 in January 2015. Erik Drost / https://creativecommons.org/licenses/by/2.0/deed.en.

12. Irving seeks to elude Thunder standout Russell Westbrook during a Cleveland win in January 2015. Erik Drost / https://creativecommons.org/licenses/by/2.0/deed.en.

13. Seen here in October 2016, this billboard in downtown Cleveland honors the talent of Irving during the second era of LeBron James. Erik Drost / https://creativecommons.org/licenses/by/2.0/deed.en.

14. Indiana Pacers point guard Jeff Teague tries in vain to keep up with Irving during a February 2017 battle won by the Cavaliers in Cleveland. Erik Drost / https://creativecommons.org/licenses/by/2.0/deed.en.

15. Irving is full speed ahead as he prepares to pass against his old Cleveland teammates during his Celtics debut in October 2017. Erik Drost / https://creativecommons.org/licenses/by/2.0/deed.en.

16. Former teammates are rivals during the 2017–18 season opener as Irving, now wearing Celtics green, tries to guard superstar LeBron James. Erik Drost / https://creativecommons.org/licenses/by/2.0/deed.en.

12 Swan Song in Cleveland

What will always be rightly remembered about Kyrie Irving's 2015–16 season is the shot heard 'round the world—the round world. Makes sense. The bomb that beat Golden State is considered by some the biggest in NBA history. If any Cavaliers fans asked him, "What have you done for me lately?" he could reply, "I won you a championship." The last memories are the most lasting memories.

What was forgotten is that Irving struggled in the regular season with injuries, personal problems, and the worst statistical performance of his career. He averaged fewer than 20 points a game for the first time since his rookie year and hit a career-low 32 percent from three-point range. His .448 overall shooting was his second-worst and his 4.7 assists per game was rock bottom. He slid in and out of his groove offensively, even in the finals, before peaking at the right time.

Some believed that Irving had the potential of leading the team in scoring the following year despite the continued presence of LeBron James. But would Irving ever morph into a traditional point guard? That ship had sailed. Coach Tyronn Lue encouraged Irving to play to his strengths. After all, James, who boasted with justification that he could thrive at every position, embraced the role of chief distributor. That allowed Irving to play the part of black hole despite irking teammates on occasion. He most often had no intention of passing the ball once it was received.

Irving had proven in the NBA Finals the efficacy of such an offensive arrangement. And when the Cavaliers hoisted their first championship banner before their season opener against the Knicks, he shared the moment with the man who continued to mean more to him than any other. He huddled with his father Drederick, and then spoke about the experience and how his career journey has strengthened their bond.

"We just have a very unique relationship which goes deeper than almost life itself," Irving said. "It was just the culmination of a lot of emotions. As a kid, kind of watching him sacrifice as much as possible to allow me to have the freedom to play basketball. But also understanding how basketball correlates to life and vice versa. And how he always related it back to me just being an even better man. It was just a total one-eighty, thinking how far we both have come."

Irving picked up where he left off that fall. Comparatively healthy at last, he exploded out of the gate, averaging 25 points on 51 percent shooting over the first fifteen games as the Cavaliers bolted to a 13-2 record. He opened the season by scoring 29 despite a blowout of the Knicks that allowed him to sit through the fourth quarter. He displayed his full cache inside and out in a promising season debut that seemed to justify his role as a scoring guard.

"Like I've always said since I've taken over, Kyrie is unstoppable," Lue said after the impressive opener. "I don't think one defender can guard him. In the pick-and-roll he's unstoppable. He has no offensive weaknesses. So, for this team to be successful, I need him to be a scorer. I need him to be in attack mode at all times. You can see, when he scores, how the game just opens up."

That is, his offensive game. His defensive game had yet to approach mediocrity. In fact, it regressed from poor to horrible. Rather than working to right a defensive ship that sank to a miserable twenty-ninth in the NBA he helped steer it aground. Ball handlers glided down red carpets to the basket. Perimeter shooters found the time to line up open shots. Passers coming off pick-and-rolls hit unchallenged teammates for easy hoops. And Irving was greatly responsible. He ranked 188th among 224 guards with a 109.7 defensive rating that season, the third worst among NBA guards that averaged at least thirty-five minutes per game and 33rd out of 42 that played thirty minutes per game. He was also dead last among Cleveland starters.

That a player boasting the level of athleticism of Irving could rank among the worst defenders in the league led analysts to search for reasons. It has been stated correctly that superior defense is greatly a reflection of intensity and desire, especially among players such as Irving with the physical gifts to excel. He had made albeit minor strides on that end of the court in previous seasons and had performed well enough defensively to outshine Stephen Curry in the NBA Finals. One can only surmise that his growing disenchantment with the Cavaliers and sharing the floor with James played a significant role in his increasing indifference as a defender.

The advanced analytics that have permeated the sports scene in recent years were not kind to Irving—and they did not merely refute any claim of defensive prowess during his last season in Cleveland. His penchant for shooting at the expense of player and ball movement weakened the efficiency of his teammates, including James. That lack of effectiveness was reflected in his true shooting percentage, which takes into account field goals, three-pointers, and foul shots. The presence of Irving did not make James better, unlike other premier point guards with standout teammates that year. Kevin Durant's true shooting percentage skyrocketed from .619 to .672 when sharing the court with Curry. That of Bradley Beal rose from .571 to .596 with John Wall on the floor. But James managed only an increase from .628 to .632 alongside Irving. Such a reality hurt the team given that Irving attempted 117 percent as many shots per 100 attempts as the outrageously efficient James.

Basketball analyst Brady Klopfer used such statistics to evaluate the overall production of Irving as an NBA player. Among the other numbers he tossed out was the 1.10 points he allowed per possession while defending the player rolling to the hoop in the pick-and-roll. Klopfer wrote the following in a July 2017 article that criticized Irving's lack of awareness of defensive fundamentals:

> It's not just Irving's ability to play on that end of the floor, it's his lack of knowledge and scheme. Watching Kyrie defend the pick and roll is akin to watching a Labrador when three balls are thrown in three directions: his head is on a swivel, he bounces and twitches, but he ultimately has no idea where to go. While most poor defensive point guards are simply bad in isolation, or off-ball, Irving constantly puts teammates in poor situations by showing no understanding of when or even how to switch in the pick and roll.

Advanced metrics were not kind to Irving in his sixth season, one in which he should have been taking steps in a positive direction as a complete player. One indicator was real plus-minus, which measures how much better or worse a team performs with a particular player on the court. Irving ranked just thirteenth among point guards in 2016–17 and forty-third overall. Even when defense was removed from the equation, he ranked eighth at his position. Such standings certainly explained why Irving again could not land a spot on even the third all-NBA team.

They also begged the issues of stardom, greatness, and effectiveness. Outrageous offensive talent, as well as the guts and confidence to rise to the occasion on the biggest stage, inspired media attention that had made Irving a star. But does that constitute greatness? In the modern era, with its emphasis on flash and attracting the spotlight, perhaps. But Irving had yet to earn real greatness, an effectiveness in all aspects of his game that he should have achieved by then through hard work and dedication. Some players simply don't boast the physical tools to excel defensively or maximize the offensive potential of their teammates. Irving had no such excuse.

So his numbers rose and his team fell, at least in the regular season. After peaking at 28-8, the Cavaliers managed a 23-23 record the rest of the year, an inexcusable mark considering the relative health of the Big

Three. They had become arguably the worst defensive club in the NBA, performing at times with an appalling apathy that led to defeats such as 117–99 to Chicago, 120–92 to Miami, 108–78 to the Los Angeles Clippers, and 103–73 to San Antonio. It was as if the Cavaliers simply didn't care about the regular season. Irving was far from the only culprit. Love spoke a year later about the disease inflicting the team that seemed to be a reflection on Lue's motivational abilities, though some believed the players followed James's lead.

"We were not good in the third quarter," Love said. "We were super-complacent. I can't tell you how many games we would have won if we had the same ball movement and player movement in the third quarter as we did in the first half." Love added that he would "stand on the perimeter" and watch what was going on, which was mostly James and Irving in isolation.

Meanwhile, Irving kept wowing and scoring. He averaged career-bests (through that season) in points per game (25.2) and shooting percentage (.473) while rebounding from an off year from beyond the arc to nail 40 percent of his three-point attempts. He even produced his best-ever effort from the foul line. But his defense was terrible and, despite a seemingly inexplicable seven-game stretch in late December during which he proved his distribution potential by dishing out 70 assists, he continued to embrace his me-first philosophy. He tossed up a career-high 19.7 shots per game compared to 18.2 for James, whose offensive efficiency remained virtually unmatched among NBA players.

If Irving knew that the 2017 playoffs were his last roundup in Cleveland, he certainly went out with guns blazing, particularly in the opening series against the surprisingly tough Pacers, who were outscored by just 16 points in a four-game sweep. Irving jacked up an average of 23 shots per game—never mind that he was cold from the field. Most unconscionable was his penchant for firing three-pointers despite his massive struggles from deep. He jacked up thirty-two in the series and hit on just seven. He nailed just 33 percent of his total attempts in the two road games. Granted, Lue, since he took over the coaching reins, had encouraged

Irving's aggression; and shooters must shoot to emerge from slumps, but this was ridiculous. He froze out his teammates in the series, compiling a mere three assists per game. And for the first time that season, he finished a game with zero assists. The Cavaliers polished off the Pacers despite his middle-of-a-bagel in Game 4.

Highly respected forward James Jones, who landed a front office position with Phoenix in the off-season, spoke that summer about the situation in Cleveland during the playoffs and Irving's apparent disenchantment with his teammates. Jones told ESPN beat writer Dave McMenamin that Irving did not speak to his teammates during practices between the first-round series and the upcoming battle against Toronto. Personal differences and situational discontent often arise during the regular season, but should be put aside during the playoffs, when teams must become a band of brothers. Irving, who had either not fully developed or hidden his dissatisfaction during the 2016 postseason run to the championship, had become the broken link in the chain a year later.

His shooting woes worsened in the second-round sweep of the Raptors and what promised to be a spirited battle against point guard rival Kyle Lowry until an injury sidelined Lowry after two games. Irving hit just 37 percent from the field but averaged nearly 9 assists per game as he switched roles with James, who became more of a prolific scorer. One wondered without a shift in mind-set and motivation how his assist total could rise so dramatically from one series to the next. Irving talked a good game about dedication to expanding his skill set and seeking to shed his reputation as a one-dimensional player while learning from others.

"It's definitely been picked apart since I've come into the league," he said about his lack of assists. "For me personally, I've just always felt like taking over the game came from literally putting the team on my back and going out there and trying to score as many baskets as possible. But there are so many more facets of the game you can be better at. Understanding that you can be effective on the defensive end as well as coming off screens and giving yourself up and sacrificing yourself up to get an even better shot for one of your teammates."

That Irving was just gaining such an understanding in his sixth season in the NBA seemed quite a stretch. And after the sweep of Toronto, he reverted to form. The difference against Boston was that his accuracy returned while temporarily tempering his proclivity for overshooting. Irving opened the series with a 4-for-11 performance to extend his slump, then buried an incredible 67 percent (42 of 63) of his shots, including 15 of 27 from beyond the arc, the rest of the way as the Cavaliers advanced to a finals rematch against Golden State.

Whether the result of his teammates' offensive malaise, his own self-ishness, or a combination of the two, Irving lapsed back to the style of play he seemingly embraced in the first round. The Warriors exploited on defense all the issues that drew criticism of both him and his team—too much isolation and not enough ball or body movement. Irving took 45 shots in two blowout defeats on the road, inspiring CBS Sports basketball analyst Matt Moore to offer the following:

> The Cavs aren't cutting, or moving, or doing anything like what the Warriors do on the weakside, and as a result, Irving isn't passing to anyone open on the perimeter. Irving's game has never been adept at that; the most common criticism of Irving is that he's not a player who sets up others, but a one-on-one scorer who looks awesome when he has it going and looks like a limited player when they don't. They're not good shots, it's not efficient offense, they're just shots he can make with his special ability. . . . Last year, the Cavaliers were able to draw space for Irving, but he capitalized. But Golden State has been better at every level on Irving. Steph Curry, with a healthy knee, is more spry and staying with him, forcing him into contested 3s constantly. They're layering the defense. They've cut off the angles. Irving's not passing, and not finishing the tough shots he's capable of.

That he did finish those tough shots back in Cleveland did make a difference, but not enough. The Cavaliers blew a late lead in Game 3, but Irving's accuracy could not be blamed. He exploded for 38 points on 16-of-29 shooting, then scored 40 on a 15-of-27 effort two nights later as his team staved off the elimination that was nevertheless inevitable. Golden State completed its avenging of the 2016 finals on June 12, 2017, in what would prove to be Irving's final game in a Cleveland uniform.

The numbers were all too familiar. Irving had unloaded more than 24 shots and managed just 4.4 assists per game against the Warriors. And his defense proved pathetic. His defensive rating of 123.0 in the series ranked third-last among all Cavaliers players and his defensive win share of minus-0.3 placed him second from the bottom. Granted, James and Love also struggled against one of the most high-powered offenses in NBA history, one that had added explosive Kevin Durant in a highly controversial free-agent signing in the off-season. But Irving ranked lower than the other members of the Big Three in defensive efficiency.

His days as a Cavalier were numbered. But they did not end before he uttered a seemingly inexplicable falsehood that drew universal attention and strengthened his reputation as one of the most enigmatic figures in American sports.

13 Say What?

Kyrie Irving never claimed that three plus three equals seven. Or that the sun is cold. Or that apes devolved from man. But he might as well have.

Irving opened a thousand cans of worms in mid-February 2017. That is when he offered to the people of the spherical world that the world is flat. He voiced surprise that his ridiculous backing of the belief—disproved five hundred years earlier by voyages embarked by the likes of Christopher Columbus and Ferdinand Magellan and most recently asserted by nitwitted conspiracy theorists—garnered so much attention. Most shocking was that it was uttered by a learned, thoughtful, intelligent man such as Irving. He also spoke about freedom of thought in questioning the validity of the moon landings and claiming the CIA tried to assassinate reggae legend Bob Marley for his desire to bring people together. He provided an impassioned view of the need for acceptance among all people inhabiting the planet and his desire for reporters to delve beyond his life as a basketball player. But only his flat-earth claims were strongly disseminated by the media, because they were so outrageous.

The only explanation in the minds of many was that, despite his expressed wonderment at the overwhelming media reaction, that was his intention. But one never knows with the mysterious Irving. If he did not truly believe the earth was flat, he certainly played a good game.

Ignorant words are most often spoken by ignorant people. Nobody with an understanding of Irving could have placed him in that category, which is why his utterances came as a shock. Irving made his puzzling claim on an airplane while recording a podcast of *Road Trippin' With RJ and Channing*, which was hosted by veteran Cavaliers teammates Richard Jefferson and Channing Frye. "This is not even a conspiracy theory," he said. "The earth is flat. The earth is flat . . . It's right in front of our faces. I'm telling you, it's right in front of our faces. They lie to us."

That Irving stated it's "not even a conspiracy theory" and "they lie to us" in the same thought process should have motivated him to offer no more than a day later that he was just joking, and all would have been forgotten. He cited "they" often during his verbal ramblings without explaining who "they" were. And he doubled down on the flat-earth nonsense soon thereafter, urging people to waste their time by delving further into it.

"I think people should do their own research, man," he told ESPN. "Hopefully they'll either back my belief or they'll throw it in the water. But I think it's interesting for people to find out on their own. . . . I've seen a lot of things that my educational system has said that was real that turned out to be completely fake. I don't mind going against the grain in terms of my thoughts."

Irving really went to town the next day in a convoluted statement during which he talked about how those who inhabited the supposed flat world were reacting to his comments, as well as his delight that they could spur conversation.

"I think there's just so much, I guess—I don't know if you can even call it news—there are so many real things going on, actual, like, things that are going on that's changing the shape, the way of our lives," he said. "And I think it sometimes gets skewed because of who we are in the basketball world and, 'Oh man, what does he actually think? Oh, no, I don't like hearing . . . the world is flat, or he thinks the world can't be round.'

"You know, I know the science, I know everything possible—not every-thing possible—but the fact that that actually could be real news, that people are actually asking me that—'It's a social phenomenon. What do you think about it? Are you going to try to protect your image?' I mean, it really doesn't matter. It really doesn't matter. The fact that it's a conver-sation? I'm glad that it got people talking like this: 'Kyrie actually thinks the world is flat.'"

What Irving might or might not have understood was that nearly all conversations revolved not around the shape of the earth, but about how a bright guy like him could question it. But the media did take the ball and run with it. They did not give credence to the flat-earth belief, but they gave credence to Irving. Some delved deeply into his psyche to justify his claims. Others praised him for thinking outside of the box. Among those that took the former approach was Ben Rohrbach, who wrote the following on the *Ball Don't Lie* website:

So, here's my latest theory on Irving's flat-Earth theory: He's into the idea of a transcendent mind or a consciousness that lives outside of the brain. In his eyes, we are not of this world. Maybe we're all in the Matrix. Maybe this is all a dream from which we'll wake up someday. That would explain a lot about the current state of the world, actually. Whatever the case, our individual world is what we make of it, and that transcends science and everything we've learned about planets orbiting space.

Rohrbach eventually changed his tune. He opined that the strange views of the twenty-five-year-old superstar were based on less cosmic, intellec-tual inspirations and more on the conspiracy theories flooding the internet, which Irving later admitted being true. And Irving was just warming up. He provided a further explanation in a podcast conducted by wildly successful University of Connecticut women's basketball coach Geno Auriemma, during which Irving tried to legitimize his cockeyed theory.

"The whole intent behind it, Coach, it wasn't to bypass science," he said. "It wasn't to like have the intent of starting a rage and be seen as this insane individual. When I started seeing comments and things about universal truths that I had known, and I had questions. I don't necessarily tell, I won't sit here and say that I know. And when I started actually doing research on my own and figuring out that there is no real picture of earth. Like, there is not one picture of earth. We haven't been back to the moon since 1961 or 1969. It becomes like a conspiracy. . . . You're like, 'Okay, let me question this.' The separation that I can't stand is because I think one particular way . . . then there's a tirade of comments of who I am character-wise. The only intent was for people to open up and do their own research."

One might be falsely attacking his character to state that Irving expressed his flat-earth theory to attract the spotlight or expand his brand. But the research Irving said he'd done was certainly far from boundless. After all, there were no excursions to the moon in 1961. And astronauts completed six moon landings between 1969 and 1972. Most egregious was his claim that no pictures of earth exist. He either did not bother learning about NASA images that prove the roundness of the planet or associated them with a giant conspiracy.

Irving spoke often about that conspiracy, but never theorized about motivation. What, after all, would thousands of scientists worldwide, NASA, and government officials have to gain by spreading lies about the shape of the earth? He skirted the question answered five hundred years earlier regarding Earthlings falling off a flat planet. To 99.9 percent of the world's population, that the earth is round is as proven a fact as one plus one equals two. But Irving, apparently inspired simply by the notion of questioning what has been universally accepted, continued to spread nonsense.

"He's a very weird duck," offered *Cleveland Plain Dealer* columnist Bill Livingston. "I assumed it was one of those jokes that he felt was funny and nobody else did. Richard Jefferson always talked about wanting to hear the latest crazy conspiracy theory of Kyrie Irving. The stuff he put out was just batshit nuts, that the moon landing was fake and that the earth is flat. I never knew whether to take him seriously or not."

Some might offer that his words were not harmless. They believe that such claims were irresponsible and came with consequences for the youth of the world, especially those who idolize NBA stars and might have embraced his ridiculous views to question their own educations.

Not all of Irving's offerings fell under the category of conspiracy theories. Others proved more thoughtful and struck a more political, religious, and social chord. He spoke about his rejection of Christmas as a valid holiday, which showed that he perhaps had evolved in his religious thinking from the time early in his career when he carried a Bible with his name embroidered on it that had been given to him by the mother of a high school teammate. He talked about planning an anti-capitalist, self-sustaining community that devalues money and promotes equality. He had become a bit of an idealist. Agree or disagree, those opinions were just that. They were not disputing scientific facts.

But the views Irving expressed that doubted what was accepted, including the very existence of dinosaurs, garnered the most attention. Most perplexing, even disturbing, was that some in the media lauded his nonconformity. Among those who praised Irving was GQ writer Nathaniel Friedman, who perceived his admittedly false claims as a reflection of an enlivening personality. Friedman wrote the following in his assessment of the phenomenon:

> It's refreshing that an athlete feels comfortable speaking this freely, and both entertaining and disconcerting that this is what comes out of his mouth. We often praise athletes who are "unfiltered," or at least ogle them approvingly; Irving is something else altogether. In giving him free rein, we've convinced him that every stray conjecture and errant line of thinking is worth verbalizing, that whatever he thinks is automatically good content. . . . We've created a monster through a combination of vague disapproval, morbid curiosity, and a perverse desire to see sheer anarchy loosed upon the nba. Irving is perceived as a crackpot, or maybe just a goofball. He's an oasis of weirdness that's all too rare in professional sports. But what if Kyrie is the last sane one in a world that's gone completely mad?

That last sentence was where the realm of logic leaked into the world of delusion. Questioning the roundness of the earth or existence of dinosaurs is sane and accepting them as facts is mad? And Friedman didn't stop there. He admitted that Irving "rambles, contradicts himself, rarely presents a real argument." But he criticized those that dismiss Irving, stating the following:

> We do so to assuage some deep-seated cultural anxieties around the concept of truth. There is no truth, or least one single agreed-upon version, in American public life these days. That's a hard pill to swallow for anyone who has staked their personal, political, or professional life on Getting It Right, the faulty assumption that having the correct answer or being the smartest person in the room is a substitute for real power. While post-truth society can be disturbing, it's entirely a fact of life. Viewing it as a crisis or bemoaning the death of The Real isn't just an unhealthy, counterproductive fetish. It's grief for a thing that never was, or at least never should have been relied on so heavily. And it's high time we left it behind.

One could perceive Friedman as espousing that Irving should be taken seriously because his conspiracy theory views are a negative reflection on modern society. But truth is truth is truth is truth. Irving crossed the line between the questioning of truth and the questioning of unsubstantiated claims. There is a vast difference between stating a belief of a second shooter in the assassination of President Kennedy and offering that the earth is flat. And what is post-truth society? It is post-truth because the internet and social media allow 0.003 percent of the population to embrace some cockamamie theory that dinosaurs never existed? Does that make the reality of the Tyrannosaurus Rex any less than fact?

Irving became entangled in the sticky web he had weaved but made no attempt to extricate himself when given the opportunity in an interview with the *New York Times* in June 2018. His defense became so nonsensical that it seemed impossible to decipher. He claimed that the reaction to his flat-earth theory lacked authenticity and that he yearned to "put that on the biggest stage of 'now it becomes your side vs. my side.'"—as if his side of the shape-of-the-earth claim boasted any validity whatsoever. When informed of a National Public Radio story that included the complaints of a middle-school teacher who could not convince his students that the earth was round because they believed Irving, he admitted that his words matter. Then he simply sliced off more baloney.

"History has shown even back then, our biggest scholars did think the Earth was flat," he said, ignoring the explorations that proved otherwise half-a-millennium ago. "It didn't just spark out of anywhere and then everyone just goes into their own groups. Definitely different scientists have come along that proved the law of gravity. Everything that science breeds, and you have specific scientists that are giving all this information, I wanted to open up the conversation, like 'Hey man, do your own research for what you want to believe in.' . . . Can you openly admit that you know the Earth is constitutionally round? Like you know for sure? Like, I don't know. I was never trying to convince anyone that the world is flat. I'm not being an advocate for the world being completely flat. No, I don't know. I really don't. It's fun to think about, though."

That is like saying it's fun to think about the possibility that the sun actually rises in the west. What's fun about perceiving absurd scientific falsehoods as truth? But Nike thought enough of the concept to release a Kyrie 4 shoe that he promoted in a Christmas commercial during which he referred to a flat earth as "my world." Among those that considered such folly dangerous was Yahoo Sports columnist Jason Owens, who wrote the following:

Surely, Nike sees this as all fun and games and an opportunity to cash in . . . But spreading ignorance is not okay. There's entirely too much misinformation available in this world as is. Marketing shoes to a largely young target demographic with false science as a hook is not clever or funny. It's irresponsible.

That Irving urged ordinary people with no backgrounds in the field to draw their own conclusions based on their research about a scientific fact seemed silly to those same ordinary people. And, finally, as the 2018–19 NBA season approached, Irving admitted his mistake. One can only speculate whether he ever in his own mind questioned the shape of the earth and could not escape that trap as deftly as he escaped those on the basketball court or if he truly believed in the conspiracy theory. And perhaps he felt more than a twinge of guilt for misguiding gullible students that perceived his word as truth. But the issue was put to rest—sort of—at the Forbes Under 30 Summit, during which he apologized for creating such a hubbub. What he didn't say was that the earth is round.

"What you say, what you do, and how you mean it—at the time, I was huge into conspiracies," he said. "Everybody's been there. Everybody's been there like, 'Whao! What's going on with our world?!' . . . At the time, you're like innocent in it, but you realize the effect of the power of voice. Even if you believe in that, just don't come out and say that stuff—it's for intimate conversations because perception while you're received changes. I'm actually a smart-ass individual . . . At the time, I just didn't realize the effect . . . I'm sorry about all that."

What Irving apparently did not regret was embracing the silly flat-earth notion in the first place. The intelligent people that walk this round planet—and Irving should be considered among them—must distinguish between legitimate and nonsensical conspiracy theories. But he was at least seeking personal growth, a commendable attribute given his standing in society as one of the premier professional athletes, some of whom stagnate intellectually and emotionally out of contentedness over their wealth and fame.

But Irving's dissatisfaction revolving around his career was a different matter. Critics were about to have a field day when word leaked of his demand to be traded from the Cavaliers and away from arguably the greatest player in NBA history.

14 The Great Escape

Finding truth in the motivation behind Kyrie Irving's trade demand after the 2017 season would require an FBI investigation. If only that organization hadn't been busy with such trivialities as Russian interference in the American election. The only sure thing is that he wanted out of Cleveland. But his explanations after he was sent to Boston proved so convoluted that fans and many in the media came away more confused after he spoke about it than before he uttered a word. The more he said, the less could be understood.

Did he seek a deal because he'd been insulted when the Cavaliers attempted to unload him to the Suns in June? Or did general manager David Griffin merely negotiate with Phoenix as a response to Irving's mandate? Or did Griffin initiate the conversation on his own in the knowledge that Irving was unhappy and his situation with the team was untenable?

Did an undeniable reality of playing second fiddle to LeBron James drive Irving to request a trade? Pushed into a corner by the media, Irving said that assertion was false. But every claim he made—at least those among the gobbledygook that could be deciphered—indicated otherwise.

Did the Cavaliers yearn to ship him elsewhere, leaving Irving to feel unwanted? Irving offered that view. James brushed it off as nonsensical.

The trade demand came out of nowhere, though the seeds had arguably been planted the moment The King returned to Cleveland in 2014. Irving had previously played the role of the big fish in a small pond as the premier player on a lousy team. Never mind that James promised to transform the Cavaliers from a bunch that owned the worst record in the NBA since his 2010 departure into a championship contender. Irving had barely improved the club over his first three seasons and he'd now be forced to play second banana for the foreseeable future. After all, Irving had just signed a contract extension. He claimed to have lured strong talent such as Gordon Hayward to join forces with him at Cleveland, but the James signing killed that plan.

Many believe Irving grew increasingly unhappy as a teammate, not merely because James overshadowed him on the court. Granted, James would overshadow anyone on the floor merely because of his greatness. But despite both thriving as isolation giants, James never froze out Irving, who boasted virtually the same usage rate over their three years together and averaged considerably more shots per game during the 2016–17 season despite shooting a far lower percentage from the field. Rather, teammates offered that Irving felt disrespected when James referred to him as "the kid" or "little brother." When asked if he felt James considered him a basketball equal, Irving replied that he neither knew nor cared. One can only take an educated guess as to whether he indeed resented what some interpreted as James's condescension.

James viewed the relationship as an opportunity to impart his wisdom and what is generally regarded as his basketball genius to a teammate. "I tried to do whatever I could to help the kid out to be the best player he could be, tried to help him be a better leader, a better scorer, a better floor general, a better defender, a better passer, a better leader vocally," James said. "I tried to give him as much of the DNA as I could, because at some point, when he was ready to take over the keys, I was ready to give them to him."

Perhaps that was the root of the problem for Irving. He didn't want to be in the passenger seat nor even share the driver's seat. He yearned to lead a team of his own, as he had the Cavaliers before the return of James. And if James indeed toiled to maximize the all-around performance of his younger teammate, he failed. Irving arrived in the league as a brilliant scorer. But he showed little desire to improve other aspects of his game, particularly as a defender, but also as a passer and floor general who could involve others and dictate the flow and pace of the action.

Teammates recalled an incident revolving around Irving during his last season in Cleveland that spotlighted his me-first mind-set and perhaps even his discontent with the team. It began with Tyronn Lue citing Irving for playing too slow—the coach had always stressed a fast-break, transition style. "Ky," Lue said, "I want you to play a little faster." Irving asked him why. "Because if we play faster, we get shots off easier," Lue answered. "I can do that anytime." Irving replied. To which a testy Lue referred to catch-and-shoot specialists Richard Jefferson and J. R. Smith, both of whom benefited from finding open spots on the court before defenses had time to set. "I'm not talking about your shot, I'm talking about RJ and JR," Lue said. "Well, that's [LeBron's] job," Irving said, prompting Lue to walk away shaking his head.

Irving later admitted he should have accepted Lue's request, but added that such minor confrontations are commonplace in the NBA and should not have been blown out of proportion. The incident proved to be further evidence that he and the Cavaliers were not on the same page. But if Irving owned a clear idea as to what separated their philosophies on or off the court and why he yearned to leave he either refused to express the unvarnished truth or did not verbalize it without a maddening vagueness. In typical, enigmatic Irving fashion, he stated what did not drive his desires. He never stated what did.

"Sometimes, in the search for 'the moment' you can get lost," he said. "I want to be an All-Star. Okay. I want to be MVP. Okay. I want to win a championship. I want to average this much. I want to be better than this person. I want the media to accept me this way. You start formulating all these false realities, and you realize that's not it at all. Once I separated myself from that, I started looking at things I wanted to do with my life, what would make me happy."

What would make him happy was left open to speculation. Among the theories was that he needed a fresh challenge. Byron Scott, his former Cavaliers coach, offered that Irving is among the NBA players who get bored with the status quo and require stimulation and new journeys. Griffin, whose firing by owner Dan Gilbert led to the hiring of inexperienced general manager Koby Altman and reportedly killed initial trade talks with Phoenix, stated that he could not put a finger on why Irving wanted out because there was no specific reason or point of no return.

"Everyone wants to find a silver bullet or magic bullet that made everything end," Griffin said. "It wasn't that. It was a gradual day-to-day thing of an evolution from a young guy who went from being the first pick in the draft to being an Olympic champion and NBA champion, making the biggest shot in the history of Cleveland; you evolve and change that way. . . . If he had articulated to me he was going to be traded, we would have traded [him]. . . . You're all the way in or all the way out on winning a championship."

The Cavaliers were not forced to trade Irving, who had two seasons remaining on the contract he signed in 2014. But ESPN, citing various factors, including the departure of the highly respected Griffin and his attempt to trade Irving for Paul George in a three-way deal with Phoenix and Indiana, reported that Irving threatened to sit out training camp and opt for surgery on his troublesome knee rather than play out the 2017–18 season if the Cavaliers held on to him. That convinced Gilbert that the relationship with Irving was irreparable.

James stated the following year that he felt frustrated and powerless over his inability to convince his team to hold on to Irving. One might believe that the trade added to his own doubt about the future of the Cavaliers that played a role in his decision to leave in free agency and sign with the Lakers. "Even if you start back to the summertime [in 2017] where I felt like it was just bad for our franchise just to be able to trade away our superstar point guard," James said. "A guy that I had been in so many battles with over the last three years, and obviously I wasn't a part of the communications and know exactly what went on between the two sides. But I just felt like it was bad timing for our team."

Irving indicated that James leaked the trade request. Irving said he was upset and angry when he first heard of it in the media during a family vacation in July. Yet despite the apparent discord between them, a reality that James did not dispel, he still sought to keep Irving in Cleveland. James even claimed to have spoken directly with Irving to mend fences.

Griffin understood. The former general manager followed Irving's journey from draft day through his first year in Boston. But Griffin apparently wasn't buying any explanation for the trade demand other than a desire to put a team on his back. One might argue Irving had that chance over his first three years and failed to turn the Cavaliers into a winner. But Griffin believed that such a transformation would have proven impossible given the talent level of the team at the time.

"[He] had been carrying the load offensively for a bad team . . . but hadn't been given the opportunity [to lead] yet, and just when we're gonna be good, LeBron shows up and it's his team," Gilbert explained. "So he never got the chance to take the natural progression in his career where he had to try to carry the load and see how good he could be. And he really wanted that. . . . He'd been doing it on a bad team. He wanted a chance to do it on a good team. And it wasn't about being the man—it's 'How good can I be? What am I capable of? LeBron can score; he doesn't need me to score. LeBron can make all the passes; he doesn't need me to do that. I'm not a better defender than he is.' So I think you get to the point where the fit and the need for LeBron had for Kyrie wasn't going to allow him to become Scottie [Pippen to Michael Jordan] because he didn't need Kyrie to fill the gaps, necessarily."

Such justification for Irving's motivation must be questioned. There is little proof for Griffin's assertion that James returned just when the Cavaliers were about to become a strong club, perhaps one that could reach or advance in the playoffs, even in a weak Eastern Conference. The team finished Irving's last season sans James with a woeful 33-49 record. Moreover, James *did* need Irving to score, especially when Kevin Love failed to live up to the expectations that followed his dominant stint in Minnesota. The Cavaliers would remain a team without a championship if not for Irving's prolific scoring, which included two 40-point performances in the 2016 finals. Indeed, LeBron could make all the passes, but that does not mean Irving should not have worked to improve his passing. As for defense, neither played it with much intensity, especially in the regular season. Irving supposedly embraced throughout his life a desire to become a great basketball player. And that meant on both ends of the court. Nothing that James did or didn't do as a defender should have affected that.

ESPN analyst Stephen A. Smith expressed uncertainty whether James leaked the trade demand, but added that Irving believed that to be true. The truth might never be revealed, but what is certain is that details were made public of a meeting between Gilbert and Irving, along with agent Jeff Wechsler, who stated that his client preferred San Antonio, New York, and Minnesota as destinations. And that did not inspire Irving to turn any cartwheels.

"I had a talk with Dan [Gilbert] in the most professional way possible," Irving said. "I expressed my feelings, and we had a genuine conversation about what was next. I thought there would be a sense of confidentiality on everyone's part. I'm not going to point fingers, even though I know fingers will be pointed anyway, but the way it happened was disappointing. It was hurtful how it spun out. It turned into a narrative where everyone got to have an opinion on why I should do this, why I should do that. I'm this. I'm that. I'm selfish. That's fine because that's not reality. It was just a bunch of noise."

What many perceived as a bunch of noise was Irving's reasoning for his trade request. In a wide-ranging interview with ESPN's "First Take" soon after the deal with Boston was consummated, he had a chance to explain it. After offering that he owed nobody an explanation, including

James, he launched into one that left viewers scratching their heads and aching for specifics.

"I don't think you owe it to another person in terms of figuring out what you want to do with your life," he said in response to why he did not consult James about his desire to leave the Cavaliers. "It's not anything personal. I'm not here to tirade anybody. I'm not here to go at any particular person or organization because I have nothing but love for Cleveland. . . . It's just there comes a time when you mature as an individual. It's time to make that decision. There's no looking back from that standpoint. There is no time to figure out how to save someone's feelings when ultimately you have to be selfish in figuring out what you want to do. It wasn't about me not wanting to win. It wasn't about that. I want to be extremely, extremely happy and perfecting my craft. That was the only intent I have in all of this."

The more he spoke, the more it became clear that he had grown disenchanted with playing for the Cavaliers and serving as merely a prince alongside The King. Trying to lure those thoughts out of his mouth turned the media into a modern-day Captain Ahab seeking in vain to track down the white whale.

15 Speaking and Saying Nothing

The media needed an Irving-to-English dictionary in the summer of 2017 and beyond as they studied his words to extract any meaning that would allow them to grasp just why he wanted out of Cleveland. Few athletes have offered less by saying more than did Irving following the swap to Boston.

The enigmatic superstar did not voice to reporters his desire to be traded, leading to speculation as to how his demand had been leaked, but he certainly opened up after the transaction was consummated. The request and resulting deal rightfully earned the distinction as the biggest story of the off-season, and the sports media wanted answers. Why would anyone benefiting from the on-court unselfishness and incredible talents of LeBron James want to bolt? Why would a player who valued championships over early vacations seek to leave a team that had reached four consecutive NBA Finals and provided Cleveland its first major sports title in fifty-two years? Why would Irving yearn to go elsewhere when he was averaging more shots per game than arguably the greatest player in history?

Such questions were indeed speculative, but future events proved that if Irving indeed no longer wanted to play alongside James, he wasn't alone. NBA analyst Brady Klopfer of the Athletic explained.

"I don't think anyone will ever know, but there are lots of factors to consider," he said. "James is one of the most respected players in the league, yet in the summer of 2018 it came out that neither Kawhi Leonard nor Jimmy Butler—marquee, elite players—were interested in playing with him. James's shadow is not like other superstars'. The media circus that follows James is insane, sometimes hundreds of reporters in your locker room after every single game, with every moment of every game under a microscope. It's incredibly exhausting. Beyond that, James is the top dog at a level rarely seen in sports. He has a say in organizational decisions, is the story of the team no matter what his teammates do, and controls the vibe, energy, and ambiance of the team, the practices, the locker room, and the games. Things are done James's way, not because he's hyper controlling, but because that's what happens when one of the three greatest players in NBA history is playing. I have no idea why Irving didn't want to play with James, but there are a lot of understandable reasons. James is one of the greatest players ever, a tremendous teammate, and a stellar person, but being his teammate is a lot. It's not for everyone."

Once the die was cast, and if indeed there is truth to the claim that Irving planned on opting for knee surgery and sitting out the season, the Cavaliers still faced palatable options. They could have traded him anywhere despite his targeting of San Antonio, New York, and Minnesota—Miami was also reportedly on his list of desired destinations.

There was certainly no lack of suitors. Twenty teams reportedly contacted the Cavaliers and six made offers for Irving, including those for which he yearned to play, as well as the Clippers and Suns. The others expressed only cursory interest, often due to a lack of assets to make viable proposals. With James still in uniform and the Cavaliers unsure if he would stick around beyond the coming season, the goal was to replace Irving not only with talent that could help maintain their standing as a title contender. Gilbert and Altman were realistic. They understood the possibility of The King leaving, so they also sought draft picks that would hasten a rebuilding process if he did.

Rumors ran rampant. One had Minnesota trading to Cleveland the same Andrew Wiggins that the Cavaliers drafted first overall in 2014 and dispatched to the Land of 10,000 Lakes for Love in luring back James. Another had the Knicks offering just about anyone but promising big man Kristaps Porzingis, but their sorry roster boasted no other player or combination of players worthy of discussion in a deal for Irving. More intriguing were the Heat, who were supposedly willing to send top talents Goran Dragic and Justise Winslow to Cleveland, and the Suns, who dangled explosive Eric Bledsoe as a replacement at point guard but refused to include budding standout forward Josh Jackson.

Soon another candidate emerged—one that desperately wanted Irving. And that was Boston. It quickly became apparent to the Cavaliers that the Celtics were the most beneficial trade partner despite their status as a threatening Eastern Conference rival. Every asset offered potential to help the team contend for a championship or, if James indeed bolted, still keep it strong. The most significant piece was diminutive point guard Isaiah Thomas, whose massive defensive deficiencies were offset by his ability to put points on the board (sound familiar?). Thomas had finished second in the NBA in scoring the previous season at nearly 30 points a game. Also offered by Boston were small forward Jae Crowder, who had emerged as a full-time starter the last two years, promising young center Ante Zizic, and the first-round draft pick of the expectedly woeful Brooklyn Nets that the Celtics had acquired. Soon the deal was done, though the Cavaliers were able to secure a second-round selection as well when it had become apparent that Thomas would lose half the season to a lingering hip injury.

The blockbuster of a deal resulted in Irving fielding tough questions about his motivations and relationships with James and the Cleveland front office. Most in the media simply nodded their heads and read between the lines to cut through the baloney. Among the most noteworthy interviews was one conducted by ESPN "First Take" analysts Stephen A. Smith and

Max Kellerman, during which a prickly Irving rambled on without saying anything concrete.

"The actual story line of everything that was created from a variety of sources, a variety of people—whether it be from my circle, whether it be from anywhere else—the last person that everybody kind of forgot about was me," Irving said. "I didn't say a damn word . . . I don't really have an ego. I have a presence and aura about me that's very reality based."

Critics might have claimed that Irving set a record for the most debatable utterances ever in the shortest span. No athlete with the desire to attempt game-winning shots, including the one that could make or break a season, is without ego. And would anyone sans ego brag about his presence and aura? And reality based? Was that really coming from a man who very publicly questioned the roundness of the planet and the existence of dinosaurs?

Irving's words became even more convoluted when confronted with the consensus claim that his desire to leave the Cavaliers was based on dissatisfaction over sharing the court with James, one of only a few players in the NBA more productive with ball in hand (as a brilliant passer and higher percentage shooter). When Kellerman asked him about a perceived unhappiness over playing second fiddle behind James, Irving claimed to not understand the concept. He also expressed wonderment that it became a huge story even though no superstar NBA teammate has issued a trade demand that would separate him from another since Shaquille O'Neal asked to leave the Lakers and Kobe Bryant in 2004.

"It's not about wanting to or not wanting to [play with James]," Irving replied to Kellerman. "It really just became how everybody turned this into a madness because it was myself and LeBron. If this were anybody else being traded, I don't think it would have been this big story line. . . . When you get to that crossroad in your career and in your life and you have to make that decision, it's not about necessarily figuring out what the other person's intent is, it's figuring out what your intent is. When I came to that crossroad and I looked at myself in the mirror and I said this was absolutely something that I wanted to do, it didn't have anything to do with not wanting to play with the best player on the planet. It didn't have anything to do with not wanting to be the second fiddle. . . . I have no idea what that is. Or being a second banana. I don't have any idea what that is."

Kellerman tried to decipher Irving's cryptic answers to questions about his relationship with James. "That makes me think that maybe there's something personal going on behind the scenes that you can't or don't want to talk about," Kellerman said. "If that's the case, that's perfectly fair. 'Guys, there's stuff behind the scenes, it's none of your business,' and I respect that. So if you're saying that, fine. If you're not saying that, then I'd like to know what you have to say about the idea that perfecting your craft seems to be, at this moment, put ahead of the pursuit of a championship?"

That is when Irving became combative. "I'm sorry, Max, that absolutely made no sense to me," he said. When Kellerman offered that, like Pippen to Jordan, he was destined to be the second-best player on a team that included James, Irving reacted testily. "I just think you care entirely too much," he responded. "I made the decision as a man, and as a man over there Max Kellerman, just respect it and leave it alone."

That was all ESPN analyst Will Cain needed to hear. He lashed out at Irving, whom he believed had taken Smith and Kellerman for a ride without strong enough consequence. "I don't want to slam anyone. It's just not what I want to do," Cain said. "But, it's not my job to hope these guys like me, that I try to encourage friendship on these programs. No, it's my job to tell the truth, and the fact of the matter is . . . that Kyrie Irving yesterday brought out a wheelbarrow full of B.S., took out a shovel, and threw it on this table, and expected you three [including host Molly Qerim] to eat it up with a smile. He condescendingly looked at all of you, especially you Max, and suggested somehow he's above questioning."

Cain was merely warming up. "Set aside that he considers himself, apparently, some kind of philosopher king that can weave word salads around every question that you guys asked," he continued. "He contradicted himself within a matter of multiple questions. Stephen A., at one point you asked him, he said it was so hurtful that he was on his China trip and his trade request comes out, and you pressed and you said, 'Hurtful, why? From who?' And he said, 'Who cares?' Are you kidding me?

"He knows what a second banana is, Max, and that's his motivation for leaving LeBron. The truth of the matter is he's heard people like you call him a second banana. He's heard people like you call him an 'iso' player, one-dimensional, and he's tired of it, and maybe that's legit. But don't sit here and evade you, Stephen A., and condescend you, Max, about trying to understand simple questions about whether or not you wanted to get away from LeBron. State your legit, honest reasons. If you're mad at people like Max Kellerman and your career desire is to prove them wrong then just lay it out there, be honest."

If Irving indeed earned second-banana status behind James, well, welcome to the club. It could be asserted that the entire NBA had been second banana to James for a decade. Though James failed most often to win the Most Valuable Player award, he was certainly accepted as its premier talent. That the Cavaliers fell into the abyss for four seasons upon his departure, including three after Irving arrived, then reasserted themselves as a four-time conference champion immediately upon his return, spoke volumes of the comparative worth of the two stars.

Perhaps if Irving had worked more diligently and passionately on aspects of his game beyond ballhandling and finishing, the accolades would have followed. If he had emerged as a Russell Westbrook type who could pile up both points *and* assists, first-team recognition would have followed. Playing alongside James did not preclude Irving from earning such accolades. Heck, Scottie Pippen was chosen as one of the Fifty Greatest Players in NBA History as selected by the league in 1996. And he shared a court with Michael Jordan. So did Kevin McHale, who played with Larry Bird.

Since it had become apparent that Irving would never bring clarity to his motivation, the media were forced to guess based on verbal clues. That led to conjecture that he had grown disenchanted with a perceived negative culture surrounding the Cavaliers, which could certainly not be described as consistently toxic, but did seem to play a role in team underachievement, particularly in the regular season.

"Because I wanted to change the environment does not mean that it stops the pursuit in terms of what I want to accomplish as a player," Irving said. "It doesn't mean that I didn't want to play with LeBron anymore. It means I wanted to leave the environment that I was in currently and felt like as energy draining as it was and how it would take me for a loop in a roller-coaster ride and all the false reality that was created by a lot of different outlets, it all came crashing down at one point after we lost the last finals. All I wanted to do is continue to figure out myself, and once I did that, I was able to step up and make the decision."

Cleveland Plain Dealer columnist Livingston believed that decision was based at least partially on escaping the shadow of James for off-the-NBA-court opportunities. Though Irving had his own Nike shoe deal, started at point guard for the gold medal-winning 2016 Olympic team, and would soon take Uncle Drew to the movie theaters, the thought of stepping into the bigger spotlight certainly could have proven enticing.

"He'd realized most players' dreams of winning a championship, but that's not enough for him; he wanted to popularize his own brand," Livingston opined. "All players are like that to some extent, but Kyrie Irving took it to the nth degree as far as I'm concerned. One year after his shot that will live forever in Cavaliers lore he wanted out, he wanted to be the big man somewhere else. I find that appalling. I'm not a Pollyanna. I know what modern players are like. I've been around the NBA since 1974 and I've seen changes for the better in style of play and worse in player attitudes, but this is one of the worst things I've ever seen. There have been guys who quit on their teams and he basically threatened to do that. He was going to have knee surgery and sabotage the season if the Cavaliers brought him back. Then he was traded for a handful of magic beans."

Those magic beans looked pretty good when they were offered to the Cavaliers. The trade was universally applauded, especially considering the generally accepted belief that it was forced by Irving. Cleveland had acquired a point guard replacement with a similar skill set in Thomas, who was coming off his finest season and promised to return to action in plenty of time to learn the system, familiarize himself with his teammates, and recreate the Big Three for the playoffs. Crowder could start or at least serve as a solid rotation forward. Zizic was an intriguing prospect. And the Brooklyn pick provided hope for the future whether or not James stuck around.

Among those that praised Altman for the deal was James, who continued to refute claims that he leaked Irving's trade demand or forced a deal by expressing surprise that it went down at all. Considering his claim that he had tried to stop the Cavaliers from dealing Irving, he believed Altman had received an impressive bounty in return.

"I don't think anybody in the organization saw this coming," James said. "It was definitely a shock, but we did a great job . . . Koby [Altman] and the guys in the front office, putting together a great package for our team to be as complete as we've been in a long time. That's what I'm truly excited about."

That excitement didn't last long. Issues emerged after the completion of the deal that proved disastrous to the Cavaliers, at least that season. The most damaging was not only the persistent hip injury to Thomas that sidelined him for half the season. It was also his weaknesses as a player that were exposed upon his return. Thomas never fit in with James and his teammates, motivating a trade to the Lakers. Crowder also proved to be a mismatch in a Cleveland offensive system that stressed isolation and lacked ball and player movement in the half court. He was sent packing to Utah. Zizic showed flashes but received rare opportunities on a team still seeking a crown. And when the Nets performed better than anticipated, even the draft choice lost some of its luster, though the eighth overall pick did net gifted point guard Collin Sexton.

Not that Irving was about to embark on his season of dreams either. He was forced to do with the Celtics what he reportedly planned to do if not traded from the Cavaliers. The result was a frustrating and premature end to a once-promising year.

16 Going Green

It was August 21, 2017. The crew bringing Uncle Drew to life again, this time as a movie attraction, was filming in an Atlanta nightclub. Suddenly, film director Charles Stone heard screaming and joyful swearing. He swiveled his chair to see the source of the commotion. It was Uncle Drew, otherwise known as Kyrie Irving, sprinting through a set of doors. Irving had just been informed that the final piece to the trade puzzle, a 2020 second-round draft pick Boston agreed to send to Cleveland, had made it official. He was a Celtic.

Irving raced outside to calm himself, staring at traffic before returning to filming at the club. Those that watched him dance for the cameras believed his moves gained energy because of the joy he was experiencing. Irving's excitement could be felt by all as he told the film's cast and crew of the breaking news. The deal had been threatened after the Cavaliers demanded more in return after coming to the realization that Isaiah Thomas would not be recovered from his hip injury until midseason. Its completion served to both relieve and thrill Irving.

There was always something happening on the set with Irving. Stone often couldn't find him, as he was playing pickup basketball between takes dressed as Uncle Drew with anyone who wished to join in. That always had Stone a bit nervous. Imagine an injury to Irving that prevented him from finishing filming or even wiped out part of his NBA season. "I had to just constantly wrangle him because god forbid he breaks his ankle because he was playing one-on-one," Stone said. "But then one of the extras would be like, 'Yo, I'll take you on,' and he'd be like, 'Well, come on with it.'"

Soon Irving was preparing to take on the NBA again, this time in iconic Celtic green. The deal was a coup for Boston general manager Danny Ainge, who knew a little something about playing point guard in the NBA. Ainge was ecstatic when the deal, which he feared might fall apart, finally went through.

But before he played his first game in a Boston uniform, Irving uttered a curious statement about how he viewed his anticipated role with his new team. He indicated a desire to embrace more of a traditional point guard role, tossing in a subtle jab against a Cavaliers offensive system featuring James that he claimed did not allow him to maximize his potential. "I'm looking forward to becoming something that I've always envisioned myself being—that's being a complete point guard on a great team," he said. "I want to be able to come off pick-and-rolls and be able to dissect the defense and to be able to have guys—and this is not a knock on anyone I was playing with, but my role was completely different. It's not just this one-on-one individual that wants to go one-on-one every single time down. That's not how I appreciate the game."

Indeed, Celtics coach Brad Stevens embraced an offense revolving around player and ball movement far more than practiced by the iso-heavy Cavaliers, but it remained to be seen how easily and enthusiastically Irving would adapt to it. What the basketball world also eagerly awaited was his willingness to play defense with intensity, a significantly greater priority for the Celtics than his previous employer.

Though most considered Irving the Celtics' premier player heading into the season, Boston was certainly not devoid of talent. Ainge had signed free agent small forward Gordon Hayward, who was coming off a season in which he averaged nearly 22 points per game for Utah. Athletic Al Horford continued to improve as one of the top passing centers in the game. And the sky was the limit for young guard Jaylen Brown and rookie forward Jayson Tatum. So promising were the Celtics that many believed they would wrest the Eastern Conference title away from the LeBron-led Cavaliers.

Then there was Stevens, who had quickly become an esteemed figure among his players and, indeed, throughout the NBA. Irving spoke about Stevens in reverence, which in turn was interpreted as criticism of former coach Tyronn Lue. After Irving buried a three-pointer despite blanket coverage from defender Dennis Schroder to put away Atlanta early in the season, he commended Stevens for creating a symbiotic relationship between the two.

"There's dialogue [between player and coach]," Irving told the assembled media. "But we prepare for it. So he understands the talent that I have at that point, especially in the fourth quarter. But I also understand his brilliant mind. So when we're preparing and going through walkthrough or simulating situations, it's kind of easy to just go off one another. I'm able to see the reads and what's going to happen, and then he makes the play calls and what he sees out there. And we're just continuously building that trust with one another. So it's pretty easy."

Irving then really put the praise into high gear: "He's the man. So for me, I just try to soak up as much knowledge as possible. Just being in kind of the passenger seat and then also, it's like having a driving-school teacher. He's driving you the whole time, then he puts you in the driving seat sometimes and you're able to see the road. When you're able to bounce ideas and have that type of connection, and it's still developing, it's pretty awesome."

The mountain that Irving and his Celtics were required to climb as they began what they hoped to be a journey to an NBA title grew steeper just a few minutes into the season opener in (ironically) Cleveland, before and during which he was booed vociferously by Cavaliers fans, who could not forgive him for his trade demand. That is when Hayward was lost for the year with a broken tibia and dislocated ankle sustained after collecting a pass from Irving. The gruesome injury, caused when Hayward landed awkwardly leaping between two defenders, drew gasps from the crowd at Quicken Loans Arena and had Irving expressing regret that he tried to force the ball into his new teammate.

The loss of that teammate inspired critics to claim the Celtics were doomed to a mediocre record and battle for a playoff spot. But a variety of factors resulted in a far brighter outcome. Included were Irving's clutch play and surprisingly spirited and effective defense (which didn't last), rapid development of Brown and Tatum, all-around efficiency of Horford, and motivational coaching of Stevens. The Celtics embarked on a sixteen-game winning streak after losing their first two, emerged as the premier defensive team in the NBA and headed into the All-Star break with a 34-10 record. Among the results was that Irving earned universal praise for his efforts on both ends of the floor. He was even leading the league in steals at one point early in the season.

Irving boasted a fine 95.5 defensive rating through eleven games, even surpassing that of his team (95.9), which had established itself as the stingiest bunch in the NBA. Not bad considering that he owned a poor 106.9 defensive rating during his six seasons in Cleveland that bottomed out at 112 in his last year there. Teammate Terry Rozier offered that Irving felt less constrained and more appreciated than he had been in Cleveland. Horford opined that the changes of scenery and roles had done him wonders.

"I'm just glad that [Irving is] in the right situation for him," Horford said. "He gets to lead our team, and really the key is him always being in the right positions. One of the things that I'm looking at on film so far is that he's always in the right spots. And if he's not, he's making effort and hustle plays and things like that. Guys, we see that, and we really appreciate that. He's really taking the lead on that, and he's been great for us on the ball."

The change in uniform not only motivated Irving to play harder defensively, but it allowed a new fan base and franchise to gain an appreciation of his talents by watching him perform on a nightly basis. Among the impressed was Cedric "Cornbread" Maxwell, a mainstay of the dominant Boston teams of the 1980s. After the Celtics had run their record to 20-4 as the surprise team in the league, given the injury to Hayward, he compared Irving favorably to two former teammates and all-time greats.

"He has the best left hand of a guy who's not left-handed of anybody I've ever seen," Maxwell said. "Larry Bird was great with his left hand, but Larry signed his name with his left hand, so he was different. And Kyrie's handle is the best. I played with Tiny Archibald, and Tiny couldn't touch Kyrie. When I see Kyrie I don't think of anybody I know. . . . This dude, it's like he's walking around with the handle of a damn suitcase. He doesn't even dribble." The commendation didn't stop there. Maxwell also praised Irving for his demeanor and intelligence. "I also notice how laid-back he is. I'm on the bus with him and there's nothing pompous about him at all. He's a smart kid."

Championship-winning Boston coach Tommy Heinsohn echoed those sentiments and added his admiration for Irving's work ethic. "Watch him an hour before the game when he's out there warming up," he said. "He does something I've never seen and he does this religiously. He starts out lefty and righty, ten feet from the basket, shooting the ball off the backboard. He's been doing this I guess forever. So once he gets in there, he knows where to put it off the glass.

"In addition, he's got a personality like [recent Celtics standout Paul Pierce] and [legendary guard Bob Cousy]. He wants to be the best. He has fun playing the game. He's ever competitive. The question was whether he'd be able to integrate into a team concept. He's been great at that, and he hits the right button you need to turn it around or put it away."

What impressed Heinsohn aside from his thoughts about how Irving had adapted to a team concept had impressed observers about Irving since he entered the league. Nobody questioned Irving's offensive talents, ballhandling brilliance, and desire to maximize his effectiveness as a scorer. But it didn't take long for other aspects of his game, those that had inspired criticism, to resurface in Beantown. While he emerged from a minor shooting slump to open the season, hitting a blistering 55 percent from the field during a twenty-five-game stretch from late November through December, his assist totals dropped and he began exhibiting the same red-carpet defense that plagued him in Cleveland.

Irving boasted a defensive rating of 97 through October. It had skyrocketed to 105 by late December following a five-game stretch in which he compiled a woeful 116.9 rating that ranked 350th in the NBA during that span as for the first time that season the Celtics struggled to win. Irving played the role of Jekyll-and-Hyde depending on which side of the court he occupied. He bailed himself out with explosive offensive performances but allowed average scorers he defensed to wear out a path to the hoop or find wide-open spaces for perimeter jump shots.

Denver guards Jamal Murray and Gary Harris combined for 64 points and plus-20 on 60 percent shooting while guarded by Irving, who countered his porous defense by scoring 33 to rescue a victory. Two nights later, Jazz guard Ricky Rubio, known almost exclusively for his distributing rather than his finishing, torched Irving for 22 points on 10-of-15 shooting as he drove past his hapless defender for easy lay-ups in an upset defeat of the Celtics. What had become a fatal flaw combating screens had reared its ugly head again. Wrote Liam O'Brien of Hardwood Houdini, a Celtics fansite:

> Irving seemed dumbfounded every time he was hit with a screen, running around screens with utter confusion while being trapped by screeners as well. This mistake was fatal especially when dealing with a point guard such as Rubio, who has the ability to blaze a defense with his court vision. If you give him room, Rubio will make you pay with his crafty skill set, and pay Irving did.

Irving compiled the worst defensive rating among all Boston players on the court for more than four minutes in the following game against the tame Memphis Grizzlies, then gave blossoming Pacers guard Victor Oladipo and backcourt mate Darren Collison early Christmas presents a week before the arrival of Santa with his porous defense. Irving managed a team-worst 120 defensive rating in that game as Oladipo enjoyed an especially beneficial relationship with Irving as his defender in finishing with 38 points. Both Jekyll and Hyde were indeed on display again as Irving scored 30 in a taut Celtics victory.

One wondered how his defensive effectiveness could slide so dramatically and rapidly. NBA analyst Brady Klopfer of the Athletic believes the answer has several layers.

"In the first month with the Celtics, he looked a lot more engaged defensively," Klopfer said. "I wouldn't say he was good per se, but he was more competent. Unfortunately, that effort level dropped off pretty quickly. I think Irving has a path toward not being a black hole on defense, but I don't know if there's any chance of him ever being good on that end of the floor. I think, at some level, he wanted to make it clear to his new teammates, coaches, and fans that he was taking things seriously. He didn't want to just waltz into Boston after demanding a trade and play lazily on one side of the court while putting up a bunch of shots on the other. Brad Stevens's system relies on selflessness, and every component being important; the goal is for the whole to be much better than the sum of its parts. Irving knew that and wanted to make sure that the organization knew he was buying in and wasn't going to go against the organizational philosophy of the Celtics. After he was acclimated, and the team was succeeding, putting in that extra full-court effort wasn't as important anymore. It's a long season."

Irving benefited from the emphasis on defense and the system implemented by Stevens upon arriving in Boston. That was proven by advanced metrics such as defensive box plus/minus (DBPM), which estimates the defensive points per 100 possessions a player contributes above a league-average player translated to an average team. Irving compiled a minus-2.3 in his last season with Cleveland to rank a woeful 416th among all NBA players. His minus-0.7 in his first year with Boston placed him just below middle-of-the-pack. But, indeed, his defensive effort and effectiveness dropped as the season progressed.

The Celtics appeared destined to cruise into the playoffs with the top seed in the Eastern Conference after a seven-game winning streak heading into mid-January, but a four-game skid helped sizzling Toronto eventually overtake them. The Cavaliers had proven, however, that No. 1 seeds mean little in the playoffs, when teams can focus on one opponent and intensity is ratcheted up. More disquieting for Boston were indications that Irving's surgically repaired knee might require more work.

The first sign of trouble appeared in late January, when the story from Cleveland arose that Irving had threatened to undergo surgery and sit out the season if the Cavaliers did not succumb to his trade demand. The report included what appeared at the time to be an insignificant detail that Irving might need a minor procedure to ease some swelling and pain as a follow-up to the 2015 knee operation. The news indicated no imminent danger, but Irving danced around the question when asked if he still required surgery.

Irving missed three games to a right quad injury in late January and early February but continued to receive a full workload. He played on March 3 against Houston despite knee soreness, then sat out the next game against Chicago. After performing well in a win at Minnesota three nights later, he benched himself at halftime in a loss to Indiana on March 11 and reported that the knee was aching more than he was comfortable with. "We don't know what it is above general knee soreness," Irving said, "and I think that's the case, but we will go and get as much testing as we need to. . . . When I actually do get back on the floor, I want to feel the level I expect myself to play at—and be able to sustain it." He added that he preferred to take a game off than undergo a follow-up procedure to the 2015 surgery, emphasizing, "That's the last thing I want to do."

The last thing he wanted to do is what he did. Stevens claimed his absence for the next game against Washington was due only to knee soreness. Ainge confirmed on March 16 that Irving would eventually require surgery to alleviate the pain but offered that such a procedure would not be undergone until after the season and that his current inactivity fell under the category of caution rather than necessity. Irving traveled with the team to Orlando and New Orleans but did not play in either game. He continued treatment, but when he stayed back in Boston rather than travel with the Celtics on their four-game western swing, it seemed the die was cast. He underwent minimally invasive surgery on March 24 to remove a tension wire in the left knee, but his knee was pronounced structurally sound and he was expected to return within three to six weeks. The early estimate would have allowed him to rejoin the team for the first round of the playoffs. What was believed to be the worst-case scenario would have had him back for the conference semifinals.

What was believed to be the worst-case scenario was not the worst-case scenario. His surgery revealed an infection that required another operation in which two screws inserted during the 2015 procedure would be removed. It was announced that Irving would need at least four months to recover. The following Instagram message he sent on April 5 was typically deep and philosophical:

> The hardest thing to do sometimes is accept the uncontrollable things life throws at you. You try consistently to learn, grow, and prepare every day to equip your mind, body, and spirit with tools to deal with some of those things, but I feel when those moments arise they all give you a sense of unfulfillment, simply because it puts some of your professional journey and goals on a brief hold. It's simply a test of your perseverance and Will, to be present, even in the wake of what's going on. In this case, finding out I have an infection in my knee is definitely a moment that I now accept and move past without holding on to the all the what ifs, proving the nay-Sayers completely f***ing wrong, and accomplishing the goals I've set out for the team and myself. This season was only a snapshot of what's to come from me. Trust Me. "The journey back to the top of Mt. Everest continues."

Irving added a Standing Rock hashtag to the message and began the long journey back to the court. Meanwhile, his absence allowed critics and supporters to compare and contrast the Celtics with and without him. The results of their analyses proved interesting. Suffice it to conclude that those who deemed them doomed after Irving went down were forced to eat their words.

17 A Question of Value

The growth of analytics and the variety of new statistical data in all sports have allowed fans, journalists, and franchise insiders to better understand the overall value of individual athletes. The days in which NBA players were judged solely by their averages in such categories as points, assists, rebounds, steals, and blocked shots are long gone. More complex studies have been deemed less important in, say, baseball than in basketball—which spotlights interdependence between all five players on the court both offensively and defensively, thereby making it more difficult to judge individual effectiveness and performance.

The intensity and efficiency in which Boston ran the highly effective schemes of coach Brad Stevens helped Kyrie Irving compile a career-best 103.3 defensive rating in his first season with the Celtics. But that paled in comparison to those of his teammates. Irving owned the worst defensive rating on the team among those who played at least sixty games, as well as those who averaged thirty minutes per game. He ranked a decent 36th in the NBA with an offensive rating of 109.6 but some consider that disappointing given his immense talent on that end of the floor. His continued failure to fully engage his teammates placed him behind many of the premier point guards in the league, including Steph Curry, Chris Paul. Kyle Lowry, Jeff Teague, Kemba Walker, Russell Westbrook, Damian Lillard, and Eric Bledsoe.

Irving's loss to knee surgery made Boston the "great unknown" heading into the playoffs. But the odds of a Celtics championship rose considerably upon the announcement of his absence. They placed fourth in the Eastern Conference, but well behind favorite Cleveland, Toronto, and Philadelphia. Oddsmakers simply didn't believe the now-starless bunch had much of a chance to advance past the second round. And they had the numbers to back up that prediction. Boston averaged 4.1 fewer points per 100 possessions than opponents typically allowed in the eighteen games Irving missed that season. That forced the Celtics to depend even more on their lock-down defense, which improved slightly sans Irving, but not enough to offset the difference in scoring.

What fell through the cracks is that Boston began finding its groove as feisty point guard replacement Terry Rozier and the rest of the Celtics adjusted to playing without Irving. They embarked on a six-game winning streak heading into the postseason that included defeats of rugged foes Toronto, Oklahoma City, Portland, and Utah. They even scored 2.9 points per 100 possessions more than those teams typically allow, which gave them encouragement that they could beat anyone in the playoffs.

Among the natural developments without Irving beyond improved perimeter defense was stronger ball and player movement that resulted in more open three-pointers. Despite the loss of his fine 41 percent shooting from beyond the arc, the Celtics shot slightly better as a team from that range without him. Among the beneficiaries were Rozier, Horford, Brown, and Marcus Morris.

Missing, however, was a scorer on which Boston could depend. Irving not only warranted significant defensive attention but he could be counted upon when baskets were desperately needed in close games, particularly down the stretch. Despite their more balanced offense, the Celtics would miss Irving in crucial situations—that seemed to be a given. What remained to be proven was if their defense without Irving as a liability could make up the difference.

They then went out and shocked the basketball world. Boston, which averaged 104 points per game in the regular season, matched that in series defeats of Milwaukee and Philadelphia while their opponents exceeded 110 points just twice in twelve contests. They won three of their games against the 76ers by 5 points or fewer as they hit clutch shot after clutch shot and used their team defense to make stand after stand with outcomes on the line. *Sports Illustrated* basketball writer Andrew Sharp offered the following in seeking to explain the rousing success of the Celtics in the playoffs during the Eastern Conference finals:

> The playoffs are where every weakness is exposed. We saw this last year, for instance, when Isaiah Thomas's size became a much bigger liability in the postseason than it ever was during the regular season. And the absence of last spring's liabilities is a big reason the Celtics are so much tougher than expected a year later. Removing Kyrie Irving from the lineup has allowed Brad Stevens to roll with five players who can guard multiple positions and switch almost everything . . . Some of Boston's offensive success may have been a fluke along the way, but the defense is very real.

Irving, meanwhile, tried to help verbally as he could not help physically. After all, nobody in the league knew the Cavaliers' tendencies as well as he did. "He's not trying to overdo it, but he's giving you little pointers here and there, and being on the bench telling guys, 'Settle in the game, I know it's fast, but settle and take your time,' things like that," said Morris. "Here's a guy that's been here, that's seen a lot in this league, and done a lot in this league. Any little thing that he's been giving us has definitely been helping."

He didn't help enough to save the Celtics against Cleveland in a series that proved his worth as a pure scorer. Boston went cold after taking the first two games, shooting just 40 percent the rest of the way in losing four of five and a chance at an NBA championship. Irving's offensive talents and clutch pedigree was certainly missed in a backcourt that struggled against one of the worst defenses in the league. Guards Rozier, Brown, and Marcus Smart combined to hit just 39 percent from the field during that stretch and, with the Eastern Conference title on the line in Game 7, drained just 8 of 42 from the field.

One can only speculate if Irving's defensive liabilities and penchant for shooting come hell or high water, sometimes to the detriment of team offense, would have been offset by his ability to create his own shot, hit mid-range and deep jumpers, finish at the basket, and rise to the occasion with games hanging in the balance. After all, the Celtics steamrolled to within one win of the NBA Finals. Nobody could guarantee that they would have extended their season with a battle against powerful Golden State had Irving been healthy. Except general manager Danny Ainge, who could be excused when he shot back against those who claimed his team performed to its capability without Irving and Hayward.

"I get a kick out of the fact that everywhere I go, people don't think we need Kyrie or need Gordon Hayward," Ainge said. "I have a much longer memory and remember how great those guys were and what an effort it took us to get them. I also remember how great they are and how young they are still. So we need Gordon and Kyrie, absolutely need them. If this playoff run and all the series of the playoffs didn't show that, then I don't know what does. We were able to win some games and we were able to fight through some tough battles, but we're much, much better with Kyrie and Gordon."

Those who agreed feared that Irving would not be wearing Celtics green much longer, though he was locked in for the 2018–19 season. The team wanted to offer him a max five-year extension for $102 million over the summer, but that made no financial sense for Irving, who could land a deal with Boston for the same length at $188 million in free agency or $137 million if he signed elsewhere. Though some interpreted his refusal as a sign he yearned to return to his hometown and play for the Knicks or even the Nets, he tried to nip those fears in the bud by speaking positively about future negotiations with management, his experiences in his first year with the Celtics, and his desire to make up for opportunities lost due to injury.

"I'm truly grateful to be able to speak with management as well as our coaching staff," he told the media in mid-June. "And we pretty much have open dialogue with the direction we're going in, and we all feel confident that we all have something to offer here. The fact that we're even having those conversations, I'm part of it, I'm thankful for.

"I think you guys can feel my attitude is really just redemption next year. Really integrating myself with our team again and really focus on winning a championship. . . . What makes it even more exciting and the challenge is now we have a championship pedigree. They have experience, our young guys, that sometimes other young guys in the league aren't necessarily afforded. They gained a lot of experience and now it can only help us going forward."

Irving had more on his mind than basketball that summer. He was also thinking about his alter ego, Uncle Drew, whose namesake film based on Pepsi commercials he wrote and directed was about to hit the theaters. The flick not only starred actors such as Tiffany Haddish and Nick Kroll but also featured retired NBA greats Shaquille O'Neal, Reggie Miller, and Chris Webber. Irving had been interested in acting since playing a basketball player who yearned to be a chef in a production of *High School Musical* at St. Patrick's. His acting coach prepared him for taking on the role of Uncle Drew in a full-length movie.

The endeavor reminded Irving that his father Drederick had brought him up to think beyond hoops and explore other avenues in his personal and professional life. A desire to evolve, expand horizons, and feed his curiosities had always come naturally to Irving, who spoke to the *New York Times* about the connection with his father as it related to the off-the-court undertaking coming to fruition.

"He's just proud," Irving reported. "He's known for a while that I have eclectic tastes in different things. I am more willing to go into different areas and try it out. It doesn't necessarily mean success or failure—if it works or not or if the perception is great or not. It's just the fact that I'm throwing myself out there and giving myself a chance. That's how he raised me."

The time-consuming project had tested Irving emotionally, mentally, and physically while he awaited news of the impending deal to Boston. But just as he embraced his inventive side as a ball handler and finisher on the court so he enjoyed the opportunity to gain a grasp of his artistic potential in a wildly different setting. He spoke about his love for creative expression, not just in film but in music and art as well, before going into the specific challenges he experienced.

"There were definitely times on the set where it kind of got maniacal for the amount of hours we worked," said Irving. "I wasn't used to that, sixteen-hour shoot days. That was a lot. So it was an adjustment from that aspect. But I enjoyed the acting. . . . I was also dealing with an in-between stage of getting traded as well, so it was really figuring how best to divide up the time. I think I did a pretty good job of it. Balancing being a professional athlete and your side interests is definitely difficult, but it's an opportunity that was afforded to me."

Screenwriter Jay Longino first considered turning the commercial character into a film creation a bit of a stretch, but producer Marty Bowen talked him into it. "We just honed on the theme of, 'You don't stop playing basketball because you get old, you get old because you stop playing basketball.' The narrative fell into place after that," explained Longino, who knew a little something about basketball, having been a Division III standout and having played professionally.

The title role was played by Irving, dressed and made up as an elderly gentleman, who teaches the kids a thing or two about basketball and life, while lead character Dax was portrayed by comedian Lil Rel Howery. Yearning to win the pick-up tournament at legendary Rucker Park in Harlem, Dax lures Uncle Drew and Drew's older friends back to the court.

Irving, who sees himself as old school, embraced the opportunity not only to widen his professional horizons but also to play a role in a film that honors basketball players, such as his father, who graced the courts of yesteryear and still serve as tutors and inspirations. Irving even morphed seamlessly into Uncle Drew, who appeared dignified and strong rather than exaggerated and comedic. The character looked a bit like the aging basketball Hall of Famer Bill Russell.

"It's just a unique opportunity that I've taken full advantage of to add 'actor' to my résumé and with the top that it has great reception," Irving said before the release of the film. "It's an incredible family movie with an incredible story, and I'm looking forward to everyone seeing it. I've always believed in paying homage to the older generations. . . . Uncle Drew has given me inspirations in terms of being able to convey my old soul through what he is and what he embodies as a character."

Uncle Drew was indeed a movie with a message. Among the reviewers who applauded that message was Nick Allen of RogerEbert.com, who praised its genuineness and Irving's portrayal of the character. But Allen panned the film for opportunities lost in maximizing the possibilities of the cast and offering that "it's a simple concept with huge potential, and it's bungled by this feature adaptation." Allen criticized what he perceived as weak jokes and pointless plotlines, then concluded his analysis with the following criticism:

> Though it has a few big laughs, Uncle Drew mistakes its goofy pitch for a free pass to be very simple with its comedy, and sappy with its emotions. But what keeps this from totally feeling like a cheap feature adaptation of a commercial is Irving's heart as expressed through the constant witticism and near-perfect character of Uncle Drew: Irving sincerely wants to inspire the young bloods in the crowd, and through the ageless joy of basketball. But even then, a lack of cleverness dominates the frame: At the end of the movie, with a completely straight face, he tells Dax, "You miss 100 percent of the shots you don't take." That's just lazy advice, and, as further proof that this movie isn't quite sure what it should be, a quote from Wayne Gretzky, a hockey player.

The Celtics and their fans cared little about *Uncle Drew*, which earned $42.5 million at the box office as a mild surprise. Far more concerning to them was the health of Irving's knee, his impending free agency, and his fit with a team seeking an NBA championship that appeared far more likely with LeBron James hightailing it out of the Eastern Conference for sunny California.

18 A Recovery and . . .
a Reunion?

Too bad there was no lie detector handy when Kyrie Irving was asked in the summer of 2018 about the possibility of LeBron James joining the Celtics in free agency. Every NBA fan, player, executive, and reporter would have loved to know his true feelings over that prospect, which he understandably preferred not to reveal. Suffice it to say he did not yell out "yippee" and turn cartwheels around the room.

"In this business," he said, "I've experienced it all and I've seen a lot," he stated simply. "So we'll see what management does."

Not that James heading to Beantown was a hot rumor. The Celtics simply did not have the cap space to sign him. It would have required his consent of a sign-and-trade that would have forced Boston to ship valuable assets to the Cavaliers. And that he'd already decided to travel in the opposite direction to join the woebegone Los Angeles Lakers if he didn't stay in Cleveland seemed a foregone conclusion. But when Stephen A. Smith of ESPN reported that James would meet with the Celtics, the can of worms had been opened and Irving was destined to receive an inquiry or a hundred about it.

Though it can be assumed that Irving would not have been thrilled had James indeed donned the hallowed green Celtics uniform, he never uttered a negative word in public about The King or their relationship. Irving dived headfirst into the growing and heated debate centered on the contention that James, who most conceded to be the best player in the league and perhaps its finest ever, deserved to win the NBA Most Valuable Player award every year because of it. That assertion has led many to claim that the best player and MVP are not one and the same. When asked if James deserved MVP honors the previous season over winner James Harden of Houston, Irving referred to James as the "NBA MVP" and Harden as the "people's MVP" while praising James as "incredible."

Based on Boston's run to within one game of the NBA Finals, the return to health of Irving and Gordon Hayward, and James's departure to the Western Conference, one could argue that the Celtics required no tinkering heading into the 2018–19 season. Irving expressed a sense of belonging and worth as he described his relationship with Boston management. It remained to be seen if his influence in luring talent was as strong as that of Isaiah Thomas, whom he had replaced as the starting point guard. Thomas helped attract such free agents as Hayward and Al Horford while even working in vain to bring the brilliant Kevin Durant to town.

Irving claimed to have established a similar relationship with Boston management, though general manager Danny Ainge felt so comfortable with the roster that he was happy to leave well enough alone. One could justifiably claim that the return of Hayward and Irving from injury was akin to adding two top-tier free agents. The Celtics refused to deal away any key pieces to add MVP candidate and brilliant defender Kawhi Leonard. The only potential problem was that he was sent instead to premier Eastern Conference rival Toronto, which immediately placed the Raptors atop many lists of likely NBA finalists.

Irving's own future in Boston remained a hot topic throughout the summer and into the fall. Irving, however, used an interview with ESPN's Rachel Nichols and a question-and-answer session in front of Celtics fans in early October to assuage concerns that he would be heading back to his hometown of New York after the season.

"The future is very, very bright in Boston," he told Nichols. "Even if I ever try to think about that thought of going elsewhere, it would be like, 'What are you thinking? We're pretty f'ing good here . . . not just for this year, but for years to come.'"

Such reasoning seemed strange coming from a man who had demanded a trade from a team that had earned four consecutive trips to the NBA Finals and had even thanked the organization that he perceived, based on his words, to have rescued him from Cleveland. But Irving turned his praise of the franchise into a vow. During the question-and-answer session in front of cheering Celtics fans, he announced his plans to remain with the team—crestfallen Knicks supporters be damned. He displayed in the process a flair for the dramatic and an understanding of the right time and place by declaring, "If you guys will have me back, I plan on re-signing here next year."

Whether Irving was merely moved by the moment and wished to please the rabid Boston fans in attendance remained to be determined. He stated his understanding that his impending free agency would remain a story throughout the season. But former Celtics star Paul Pierce was taking him at his word.

"I think that's a legacy decision for him to see the potential of that team moving forward in Boston," Pierce said. "Winning a championship in Boston is different than winning one in Cleveland. He will be immortalized if he wins in Boston."

The number of absurdities in such a claim could have been alphabetized A to Z. Among them is that Irving drained the shot that gave the Cavaliers their only world championship—the first title for a major Cleveland sports team in fifty-two years. The Celtics, on the other hand, had won seventeen crowns and resided in a city that seemingly also hosted parades year after year for the Patriots or Red Sox or both.

And the only reason Irving might never be immortalized in Cleveland was that he demanded to be traded elsewhere, then insulted the city and its fandom. He compared them unfavorably to those of his new location during an interview with the *Charlotte Observer* before the 2017 season opener in Cleveland, a coincidence that only added fuel to the fire and turned what might have been cheers in remembrance of his title-winning three-pointer into boos by fans who now considered him a traitor.

"Boston, I'm driving in and [thinking], 'I'm really playing in a real, live sports city,'" Irving said. He also contrasted the two metropolises. Many perceived that comparison as making Cleveland seem like an Old West ghost town with tumbleweeds rolling through it. "It's exciting to be back on the East Coast," he said. "It's fast-paced. A lot of different cultures, food, and people. You get it all, especially in Boston. You would go to Cleveland, and it would be nighttime, and things would be going on, but you see a vast difference."

Though Cleveland is known for its ethnic diversity and the loyalty of its sports fans (one need look no further for evidence than the continued sellouts of Browns games for easily the worst franchise in football), one could not argue with his contentions. Boston has about double the population of Cleveland, making it naturally more bustling and livelier. But beyond his trade demand, Irving's unfortunate choice of words certainly transformed him from hero to villain in the hearts and minds of fans in northeast Ohio.

They had not forgotten a year later as Irving was about to return to the court. He made a few amends when he praised point guard heir apparent Collin Sexton, a promising Cavaliers rookie, and offered no complaint that he would be wearing Irving's familiar No. 2 Cleveland uniform. Irving even waxed nostalgic in the process as he spoke about having donned that jersey during the championship run.

"The history, it's already captured, man," he said. "I was on one of the best teams in NBA history, in my opinion, just accomplishing something that was that much bigger than ourselves. A feat that's—we're one of no other teams. We're one of one, in history [to rebound from a 3-1 NBA Finals deficit]. So, for me, I think the biggest thing is giving that jersey . . . to my dad. If that's where the No. 2 legacy ends, then cool."

His own legacy would soon be tested by how effectively he rebounded from the season-ending surgery months earlier. Irving had completed a successful treatment and recovery process that would allow him to start training camp on time. The infection discovered on the metal wiring and screws in his knee could have resulted in a staph infection, but doctors nipped that potential problem in the bud. They treated the infection by inserting a catheter into a vein going into his heart. He was also placed on antibiotics for two months.

One wondered if the knee problems that had plagued him since his Duke days would ever afford him complete health and peace of mind, but at least all seemed well as his second season in Boston approached. Most of all, he was relieved to have finished a rehab that he admitted proved to be a traumatic, even frightening experience.

Irving had overcome the third major injury of his basketball career (though the third stemmed from the second). He was prepared to move forward and perhaps fulfill the potential heaped upon him by Ainge, who offered as the season began that Irving could be the best player in the world. Then there were the words of high school coach Kevin Boyle. "He'll be an MVP," Boyle predicted. "Maybe not this year, but he'll be an MVP before he's done."

That was a heady prediction for a player who had yet to land a spot above third-team All-NBA. But in the grand scheme of things, what matters most is what matters most to Irving. He is a man of intellectualism and many interests who, despite the silliness of his flat-earth claim and questioning the existence of dinosaurs, seeks to explore for truths. His personal life revolves around love and respect for family. It's a long journey, but one he is taking with enthusiasm and curiosity. Only Irving and Father Time will determine if the isolation assassin can ever gain the motivation and passion to mature into more than a one-dimensional wonder and a mystery wrapped in a riddle.

Epilogue

Father Time has been an ally to Kyrie Irving, as it has to all NBA players in this era of one-and-done and high school graduation eligibility. The old winged guy with a long white beard, usually portrayed holding a scythe and hourglass, has provided athletes an opportunity to mature with a significant number of seasons remaining in their careers.

Despite having played seven years in the league, Irving was a mere twenty-six when the 2018–19 campaign began. He had regained relative health after knee surgery had killed any chance of his contributing to a surprising playoff run that pushed Boston to the brink of the NBA Finals. Though some wondered if the defensive tenacity and versatility that marked that blitz through the Eastern Conference would have been possible had Irving played, others believed his ability to score and rise to the occasion for a young team in the most critical moments would have resulted in a defeat of Cleveland and a clash for the crown against Golden State.

The following season started strangely and disappointingly for the Celtics. They managed a 38-26 record that placed them fifth in the Eastern Conference, ten games behind Milwaukee and eight in arrears of

Toronto—which had shown its commitment to defense by sending DeMar DeRozan to San Antonio for small forward and two-time NBA Defensive Player of the Year Kawhi Leonard. Some blamed Irving for those struggles, though he did display greater concentration on the defensive end. One wondered if that resolve would continue throughout the season, but he had forged a positive defensive box plus/minus through sixty games (though barely). And Irving showed other signs of maturity and desire to improve his all-around performance with career-highs in rebounds, steals, assists, and blocked shots. But he grew sullen and detached from his teammates as the defeats piled up, and as speculation grew that he was going to break his promise and bolt Boston after the season.

He was clearly the premier Boston player well past midseason. And he proved unabashed in voicing his views about what he believed to be wrong with the Celtics. That too represented a change for those who perceived Irving as a man more concerned with personal achievement and brand than maximizing team success. In fact, he criticized his teammates for that very thing, claiming that they were motivated to win only if accomplishing it did not negatively affect their individual agendas. Irving even exhibited uncharacteristic anger following a loss to Denver after Nuggets point guard Jamal Murray spit in the face of NBA etiquette by firing a three-pointer at the buzzer in an attempt to reach 50 points with the outcome decided. Feeling that he and his team had been disrespected, Irving grabbed the ball and launched it into the stands, motivating the league to levy a $25,000 fine. And though he stated a belief that the penalty was justified, as the ball could have hurt an unsuspecting spectator, he expressed no regret for his actions, citing that Murray had violated the sanctity of the sport.

While Irving embraced a veteran leadership role and toiled purposefully to expand his contributions on the court, he again showed a level of verbal immaturity off it that belied his thoughtfulness and intelligence. Clearly frustrated after a loss to the pathetic New York Knicks, he spoke with disdain about the upcoming Turkey Day. "I don't celebrate Thanksgiving," he said. "Fuck Thanksgiving."

Given the appalling mistreatment of Native Americans over the centuries and his visit to the Standing Rock reservation a year earlier to honor his mother, negative feelings about the holiday might be considered more understandable coming from Irving than others. But the flippant and profane comment about a universally embraced holiday in America proved highly insulting—and he knew it. Irving quickly apologized, explaining that his words were a product of frustration after a disturbing defeat.

Perhaps an act of contrition rather than doubling down on a mistake, as he had after first voicing support for the flat-earth nonsense, offered proof that Irving was gaining a sense of self-actualization that he had been diligently seeking throughout his adult life.

The promising evolution of Irving was exhibited again in January 2019, when he spoke apologetically about the criticism of his youthful teammates earlier in the season. During the interview, he recalled his own immaturity as a younger player in Cleveland and talked about having since reached out to LeBron James for advice on how a veteran leads less-experienced players to a championship. He admitted mistakes dealing with James, as well as motivation early in his NBA career toward individual statistics and awards rather than striving for team goals. Indeed, both his on-court and off-court actions in his eighth season indicated permanent growth.

Then again, maybe not. What is certain about Kyrie Irving is that you can never be certain about Kyrie Irving. That is what makes him perhaps the most enigmatic figure in American sport.

Notes

1. THE PRODIGY FROM DOWN UNDER

Pablo S. Torre, "The Making of Kyrie Irving," *ESPN The Magazine*, December 25, 2012, http://www.espn.com/nba/story/_/id/8766642/cleveland-cavaliers-point-guard -kyrie-irving-next-big-nba-star-espn-magazine.

TJ Cotterill, "Before Kyrie Irving Became an NBA Star, His Mom Starred at Rogers and Lincoln," *Tacoma News Tribune*, October 24, 2017, https://www.thenewstribune .com/sports/high-school/article180715141.html.

Find a Grave website, "Elizabeth Ann Larson Irving," https://www.findagrave.com /memorial/181826472/elizabeth-ann-irving, accessed July 2018. "Ranking Kyrie Irvings's Nike Signature Sneakers," *Sports Illustrated*, January 22, 2019, https://www .si.com/nba/2019/01/22/celtics-kyrie-irving-nike-signature-sneakers-cavaliers -lebron-james.

Tim Bontemps, "Kyrie Irving's Roots in the Standing Rock Sioux Tribe and His Wind- ing Journey Back," *Washington Post*, August 24, 2018, https://www.washingtonpost .com/sports/kyrie-irvings-roots-in-the-standing-rock-sioux-tribe-and-his-winding -journey-back/2018/08/24/701e7878-a785-11e8-97ce-cc9042272f07_story.html ?noredirect=on&utm_term=.a9af3828ad8d.

Marc J. Spears, "Irving Rewards Father's Perseverance," Yahoo! Sports, June 17, 2011, https://sports.yahoo.com/news/irving-rewards-fathers-perseverance-183900010 --nba.html.

Torre, "The Making of Kyrie Irving."

Torre, "The Making of Kyrie Irving."

Jackie MacMullan, "A Father Dedicated to Helping His Son," ESPN.com, February 24, 2012, http://www.espn.com/nba/story/_/page/kyrieirving_120224/nba-father -laid-plan-kyrie-irving-followed-it.

MacMullan, "A Father Dedicated to Helping His Son."

Brendan Prunty, "Emergence of Duke's Kyrie Irving No Surprise to St. Patrick's Kevin Boyle," *Star-Ledger*, June 21, 2011, https://www.nj.com/college-basketball/index .ssf/2010/12/emergence_of_dukes_kyrie_irving_no_surprise_to_st_patricks_kevin _boyle.html.

Torre, "The Making of Kyrie Irving."

2. RISING ABOVE THE BALLERS OF JERSEY

Mary Schmitt Boyer, "Kyrie Irving Wants to Remain Normal, but Cleveland Cavaliers' Potential No. 1 Pick Is Anything but, Say Coaches, Teammates," Cleveland.com, May 31, 2011. https://www.cleveland.com/cavs/index.ssf/2011/05/kyrie_irving _wants_to_remain_n.html.

Boyer, "Kyrie Irving Wants to remain Normal," Cleveland.com, May 31, 2011, https:// www.cleveland.com/cavs/index.ssf/2011/05/kyrie_irving_wants_to_remain_n.html.

"Montclair Kimberley 82, Collegiate 59 – Prep B Tournament," *Star-Ledger*, February 19, 2008, https://www.nj.com/hssports/results/boysbasketball/index.ssf/2008 /02/montclair_kimberley_82_collegi.html.

Clayton Geoffreys, *Kyrie Irving: The Inspiring Story of One of Basketball's Most Versatile Point Guards* (Winter Park, FL: Calvintir Books, 2017), 16.

Flinder Boyd, "Kyrie Irving, the Untold Story: From Musical-Loving Kid to Ferocious Superstar," Bleacher Report, May 17, 2017, https://bleacherreport.com/articles /2710100-how-kyrie-irving-learned-to-love-being-himself.

Tom Westerholm, "Kyrie Irving's High School Coach Believed Boston Celtics Star Would Be the Best Guard in New Jersey History," Mass Live, January 23, 2018, https://www .masslive.com/celtics/index.ssf/2018/01/kyrie_irving_boston_celtics_st_11.html.

Westerholm, "Kyrie Irving's High School Coach."

Spears, "Irving Rewards Father's Perseverance."

Boyd, "Kyrie Irving, the Untold Story."

Westerholm, "Kyrie Irving's High School Coach."

Westerholm, "Kyrie Irving's High School Coach."

Lee Jenkins, "Kyrie Irving's Burden," *Sports Illustrated*, March 5, 2012, https://www .si.com/vault/2012/03/05/106166527/kyrie-irvings-burden.

Boyd, "Kyrie Irving, the Untold Story."

Boyer, "For Kyrie and Dred Irving, a Long, Winding Road Took Them to a Magical Draft Night (and the Cleveland Cavaliers)," *Cleveland Plain Dealer*, June 25, 2011,

https://www.cleveland.com/cavs/index.ssf/2011/06/for_kyrie_and_dred_irving
_a_lo.html.

Boyd, "Kyrie Irving, the Untold Story."

3. STEPPINGSTONE TO STARDOM

Torre, "The Making of Kyrie Irving."

"Irving and Hairston Win Gold with USA U18 Team," USA Basketball, July 1, 2010,
http://www.goduke.com/ViewArticle.dbml?DB_OEM_ID=4200&ATCLID=
204964957.

Joedy McCreary, "Duke's Incoming Point Guard Kyrie Irving Settles In," High School
OT, July 16, 2010, https://www.highschoolot.com/content/story/7977046/.

Aaron Dodson, "Kyrie Irving: One-and-done to No. 1," The Undefeated, July 1, 2010,
https://theundefeated.com/features/boston-celtics-kyrie-irving-duke-2010-ncaa
-tournament-nba-draft-oral-history/.

Dodson, "Kyrie Irving: One-and-Done."

Stephen Wiseman, phone interview with author, September 18, 2018.

Michael Tomko, "Irving Stronger in Wake of Injury," GoDuke, February 5, 2011, http://
www.goduke.com/ViewArticle.dbml?DB_OEM_ID=4200&ATCLID=205089945.

Wiseman, interview.

Wiseman, interview.

Boyer, "For Kyrie and Dred Irving."

Dodson, "Kyrie Irving: One-and-Done."

Dodson, "Kyrie Irving: One-and-Done."

Associated Press, "Derrick Williams, Arizona crush Duke's Hopes to Repeat as Champions," March 25, 2011, http://www.espn.com/mens-college-basketball/recap
?gameId=310830150.

Dodson, "Kyrie Irving: One-and-Done."

4. ROCKING AND ROLLING TO CLEVELAND

Torre, "The making of Kyrie Irving."

Dodson, "Kyrie Irving: One-and-Done."

Spears, "Irving Rewards Father's Perseverance."

Brian Windhorst, "Locked Out, Shut Down: Irving's Summer," ESPN, September
23, 2011, http://www.espn.com/nba/story/_/page/irvingsummer-110923/kyrie
-irving-hard-summer.

Boyd, "Kyrie Irving, the Untold Story."

Rick Noland, phone interview with author, August 15, 2018.

Torre, "The Making of Kyrie Irving."

Associated Press, "Kyrie Irving Wins Rookie of Year," May 15, 2012, http://www.espn
.com/nba/story/_/id/7932099/cleveland-cavaliers-kyrie-irving-runaway-winner
-rookie-year.

Bill Livingston, phone interview with author, July 23, 2018.

5. STAGNATION

Associated Press, "Cavs Owner Believes Playoffs Not Far Away," May 9, 2012, https://
newsok.com/article/feed/380415/cavs-owner-believes-playoffs-not-far-away.

Noland, interview.

Jackie MacMullan, "Behind Kyrie Irving's Controversial Departure from Cleveland—
and What He Hopes to Find in Boston," ESPN, January 3, 2018, http://www.espn
.com/nba/story/_/id/21941260/nba-playing-lebron-winning-nba-title-kyrie-irving
-decided-move-question-why.

Boyer, "Cavs coach Scott Laments Loss of Irving with Broken Hand," *Cleveland Plain
Dealer*, July 15, 2012, https://www.cleveland.com/cavs/index.ssf/2012/07/cavs
_coach_scott_laments_loss.html.

Associated Press, "Kyrie Irving Breaks Right Hand," July 16, 2012, http://www.espn
.com/nba/story/_/id/8167467/cleveland-cavaliers-guard-kyrie-irving-breaks-right
-hand-las-vegas-practice.

Sam Amick, "Kyrie Irving Takes LeBron James' Role as Cleveland King," *USA Today*,
February 18, 2013, https://www.usatoday.com/story/sports/nba/2013/02/17/kyrie
-irving-lebron-james-cleveland-cavaliers-nba-all-star-game/1926431/.

Amick, "Kyrie Irving Takes LeBron."

"Dan Gilbert Admits Mistake," ESPN, April 24, 2013, http://www.espn.com/nba/story
/_/id/9206907/cleveland-cavaliers-officially-rehire-mike-brown-new-coach.

6. OLD STORY AND NEW CONTRACT

Chris Broussard, "Cavs Shopping Dion Waiters," ESPN, November 28, 2013, http://
www.espn.com/nba/story/_/id/10046614/cleveland-cavaliers-shopping-dion
-waiters.

Mary Schmitt Boyer, "Cleveland Cavaliers Guard Dion Waiters Says There Was No
Physical Confrontation during Players-Only Meeting Last Week in Minnesota,"
Cleveland Plain Dealer, November 19, 2013, https://www.cleveland.com/cavs/index
.ssf/2013/11/cleveland_cavaliers_guard_dion.html#incart_special-report.

Jordan Heck, "Kyrie Irving Regrets How He Treated Mike Brown When He
Coached Cavs," *Sporting News*, June 1, 2017, http://www.sportingnews.com
/us/nba/news/cleveland-cavaliers-news-kyrie-irving-mike-brown-relationship
/18gqnt3qvgfse10rvi2vknpk1k.

DJ Siddiqi, "Kyrie Irving Had Gordon Hayward Committed to Cavaliers in 2014," 247 Sports, July 30, 2018, https://247sports.com/nba/boston-celtics/Article/Kyrie-Irving-had-Gordon-Hayward-committed-to-Cleveland-Cavaliers-in-2014-120207833/.

Brian Windhorst and Dave McMenamin, *Return of the King*, (New York: Grand Central, 2017), 24.

Windhorst and McMenamin, *Return of the King*, 25.

"Kyrie Irving: LeBron Return 'Exciting,'" ESPN, July 20, 2014, http://www.espn.com/nba/story/_/id/11236901/kyrie-irving-excited-lebron-james-return-cleveland-cavaliers.

Noland, interview.

7. CHANGING EXPECTATIONS

Michael Rosenberg, "Eye on the Prize: How Kyrie Irving Got LeBron's Cavaliers Back to the Finals," *Sports Illustrated*, May 31, 2016, https://sg.news.yahoo.com/eye-prize-kyrie-irving-got-192449396.html.

Dave McMenamin, "Waiters: Cavs Have Best Backcourt," ESPN, September 30, 2014, https://abcnews.go.com/Sports/waiters-cavs-best-backcourt/story?id=25871688. Steven Loung, "Backcourt Debate: How Good Is Lowry-DeRozan?" Sportsnet, October 15, 2014, https://www.sportsnet.ca/basketball/nba/the-great-backcourt-debate-of-2014/. Kyle Newport, "John Wall and Dion Waiters Get in War of Words over Who Has Best Backcourt," Bleacher Report, September 30, 2014, https://bleacherreport.com/articles/2216217-john-wall-and-dion-waiters-get-in-war-of-words-over-who-has-best-backcourt.

Joe Vardon, "After a Rocky Start, LeBron James and Kyrie Irving Now See the Game Together, Their Own Way," Cleveland.com, March 31, 2015, https://www.cleveland.com/cavs/index.ssf/2015/03/lebron_james_kevin_love_kyrie.html.

Dave McMenamin, "On 'His Night,' Irving Revels in Cavs' Glory," ESPN, January 29, 2015, http://www.espn.com.au/blog/cleveland-cavaliers/post/_/id/385/on-his-night-irving-revels-in-cavs-glory.

Windhorst and McMenamin, *Return of the King*, 88.

Noland, interview.

Associated Press, "Kyrie Irving Scores 57 to Lead Cavs to OT Win over Spurs," ESPN, March 13, 2015, http://www.espn.com/nba/recap?gameId=400579256.

Vardon, "After a Rocky Start."

8. THE ECSTASY AND THE AGONY

Bud Shaw, "Kyrie Irving Shines Brightly in his First Playoff Game," Cleveland.com, April 20, 2015, https://www.cleveland.com/budshaw/index.ssf/2015/04/cleveland_cavaliers_kyrie_irvi.html.

McMenamin, "Cavaliers' Big Three Erase Playoff Doubts," ESPN, April 19, 2015, http://www.espn.com/blog/cleveland-cavaliers/post/_/id/720/big-three-erases-doubts-about-cavaliers-playoff-readiness.

John J. Kim, "Kyrie Irving Won't Use Foot Injury as Excuse for Subpar Play in Game 3," *Chicago Tribune*, May 10. 2015, http://www.chicagotribune.com/sports/basketball/bulls/ct-kyrie-irving-side-cavaliers-bulls-spt-0510-20150509-story.html.

Dan Feldman, "Report: LeBron James Called Kyrie Irving Soft Over Injury in 2015 Playoffs," NBC Sports. July 10, 2018, https://nba.nbcsports.com/2018/07/10/report-lebron-james-called-kyrie-irving-soft-over-injury-in-2015-playoffs/.

Vardon, "LeBron James, Kyrie Irving and the Conundrum of Playing Through Pain in the Playoffs," Cleveland.com, May 26, 2015, https://www.cleveland.com/cavs/index.ssf/2015/05/lebron_james_kyrie_irving_and.html.

Windhorst, "Emotions Run High after Irving's Knee Setback," ESPN, June 5, 2015, http://www.espn.com/blog/cleveland-cavaliers/post/_/id/1068/emotions-run-high-after-irvings-knee-setback.

"Kyrie Irving to Have Season-Ending Surgery on Fractured Kneecap," ESPN, June 5, 2015, http://www.espn.com/nba/playoffs/2015/story/_/id/13020515/kyrie-irving-cleveland-cavaliers-fractures-kneecap-season-ending-surgery.

Windhorst and McMenamin, *Return of the King*, 125.

9. SPREADING HIS WINGS

Chris Fedor, "Kyrie Irving Cleared by Doctors to Begin Working Out, Able to Put Pressure on Leg Following Surgery," Cleveland.com, July 25, 2015, https://www.cleveland.com/cavs/index.ssf/2015/07/kyrie_irving_cleared_by_doctor.html.

"Kyrie Irving: I Knocked Up Texas Beauty Queen," TMZ Sports, September 23, 2015, http://www.tmz.com/2015/09/23/kyrie-irving-child-support-andrea-wilson-texas-miss-texas/. "Kyrie Irving—He Left Me High & Dry & Preggo . . . Says Beauty Queen," TMZ Sports, September 25, 2015, http://www.tmz.com/2015/09/25/kyrie-irving-andrea-wilson-response/.

Chris Haynes, "Kyrie Irving Says He Has No Beef with John Wall for Saying 'It's a Joke' Irving's Second in NBA All-Star Game 2016 Voting," Cleveland.com, January 5, 2016, https://www.cleveland.com/cavs/index.ssf/2016/01/kyrie_irving_john_wall_1.html.

Tony Cartagena, "The Black Mamba Says Kyrie Irving Also Has That 'Killer Mentality.'" ESPN Wisconsin, February 11, 2016, http://www.espn.com/blog/cleveland/post/_/id/870/the-black-mamba-says-kyrie-irving-also-has-the-killer-mentality.

McMenamin, "Kyrie Irving, at Kobe Bryant's Behest, Ready to 'Step Up,'" ESPN, March 12, 2016, http://www.espn.com/blog/cleveland-cavaliers/post/_/id/2278/kyrie-irving-at-kobe-bryants-behest-ready-to-step-up.

McMenamin, "Kyrie Irving, at Kobe Bryant's Behest."

McMenamin, "Kyrie Irving, at Kobe Bryant's Behest."

Chris Haynes, "Kyrie Irving Shows Again He's Not Ready to Lead a Team," Cleveland .com, March 17, 2016, https://www.cleveland.com/cavs/index.ssf/2016/03/kyrie _irving_shows_again_that_hes_not_ready.html.

Jeff Schudel, phone interview with author, September 11, 2018.

McMenamin, "Cavs' Kyrie Irving: 'Just Crazy to Think We're Still in First Place,'" ABC News, April 1, 2016. https://abcnews.go.com/Sports/cavs-kyrie-irving-crazy -place/story?id=38097134.

10. THE RUN AND "THE SHOT"

Rosenberg, "Eye on the Prize."

William Ezekowitz, "2016 NBA Finals Preview Stat-Around," Harvard Sports Analysis, June 2, 2016, http://harvardsportsanalysis.org/2016/06/2016-nba-finals-preview -stat-around-2/.

Scott Cacciola, "LeBron James, Replying to Taunts, Takes Step Forward to Historic Comeback," *New York Times*, June 14, 2016, https://www.nytimes.com/2016/06 /15/sports/basketball/lebron-james-nba-finals-cleveland-cavaliers.html.

Livingston, interview.

"Cavs' Kyrie Irving Credits 'Mamba mentality' after NBA Finals Victory," SI Wire, June 20, 2016, https://www.si.com/nba/2016/06/20/nba-finals-cleveland-cavaliers -golden-state-warriors-mamba-mentality.

J. A. Adande, "Cavs' Historic NBA Finals and What Could Have Been," ESPN, June 20, 2016, http://www.espn.com/nba/playoffs/2016/story/_/id/16352511/cavs -historic-finals-have-been.

11. THE OFF-SEASON OF DREAMS

Boyd, "Kyrie Irving, the Untold Story."

Nathaniel Cline, "Kyrie Irving at Cavs Parade: 'I've Been Watching the Block More Than Anything,'" June 22, 2016, https://www.cleveland.com/cavs/index.ssf/2016 /06/kyrie_irving_at_cavs_parade_iv.html.

Feldman, "Report: Kyrie Irving Considered Requesting a Trade after Cavaliers' Championship Season," NBC Sports, July 22, 2017, https://nba.nbcsports.com /2017/07/22/report-kyrie-irving-considered-requesting-a-trade-after-cavaliers -championship-season/.

Noland, interview.

Andrew Joseph, "Kyrie Irving Isn't Wrong—a Gold Medal Is as Important as an NBA Championship," *USA Today*, August 10, 2016, https://ftw.usatoday.com/2016/08 /kyrie-irving-gold-medal-team-usa-nba-championship-rio-olympics.

Jack Dolgin, "NBA Star Kyrie Irving Changes Course, Puts Duke Degree on Hold Despite Previous Commitment," *Duke Chronicle*, July 26, 2016, https://www.dukechronicle.com/article/2016/07/nba-star-kyrie-irving-changes-course-puts-duke-degree-on-hold-despite-previous-commitment.

UNICEF, "NBA All-Star Kyrie Irving Visits Schools in South Africa with UNICEF," August 28, 2013, https://www.unicefusa.org/press/releases/nba-all-star-kyrie-irving-visits-schools-south-africa-unicef/8279.

12. SWAN SONG IN CLEVELAND

Steve Aschburner, "Kyrie Irving's 2016–17 Mandate: Lead Cavs in Scoring," NBA.com, October 26, 2016, http://www.nba.com/article/2016/10/26/cleveland-cavaliers-kyrie-irving-needs-score.

Aschburner, "Kyrie Irving's 2016–17 Mandate."

Brady Klopfer, "The Limitations of Kyrie Irving and the Cavaliers Building Around Him," Basketball Breakdown, July 11, 2017, https://bballbreakdown.com/2017/07/11/the-limitations-of-kyrie-irving-and-building-around-him/.

NBA Advanced Stats, NBA.com, https://stats.nba.com/players/defense/?sort=DEF_RATING&dir=-1&Season=2015–16&SeasonType=Playoffs&LastNGames=7&TeamID=1610612739.

Terry Pluto, "Cleveland Cavaliers: How Many Games Can They Win?" *Cleveland Plain Dealer*, October 18, 2018, https://www.cleveland.com/pluto/index.ssf/2018/10/cleveland_cavaliers_how_many_g.html.

Chris Fedor, "Kyrie Irving Has Added Unguardable Shot to Offensive Repertoire," Cleveland.com, May 7, 2017, https://www.cleveland.com/cavs/index.ssf/2017/05/kyrie_irving_has_added_unguard.html.

Matt Moore, "NBA finals: Kyrie Irving's Struggles Tops among Cavaliers' Woes vs. Warriors," CBS Sports, June 5, 2017, https://www.cbssports.com/nba/news/nba-finals-kyrie-irvings-struggles-top-among-cavs-offensive-woes-vs-warriors/.

13. SAY WHAT?

Road Trippin' Podcast, episode 7, "Kyrie Irving—DEEP in Thought 30,000 Feet High Above, February 6, 2017," You Tube. https://www.youtube.com/watch?v=mzjL9JxSFAk. "Cavs' Kyrie Irving on 'Earth is flat' comments: 'I know the science,'" ESPN, February 18, 2017, http://www.espn.com/nba/story/_/id/18710759/kyrie-irving-cleveland-cavaliers-believes-earth-flat.

"Cavs' Kyrie Irving on 'Earth Is Flat.'"

"Cavs' Kyrie Irving on 'Earth Is Flat.'"

Ben Rohrbach, "Yeah, so, Kyrie Irving Thinks There's 'Not One Real Picture of Earth,'" *Ball Don't Lie*, November 1, 2017, https://sports.yahoo.com/yeah-kyrie-irving-thinks-theres-not-one-real-picture-earth-193305478.html.

Andrew Joseph, "Kyrie Irving Explained Why He Thinks the Earth Is Flat: 'There Is No Real Picture of Earth,'" *USA Today*, November 1, 2017, https://ftw.usatoday.com/2017/11/kyrie-irving-earth-flat-theory-no-real-picture-podcast-geno-auriemma-celtics-nba.

"List of Six Manned Moon Landings," History Lists, https://www.historylists.org/events/list-of-6-manned-moon-landings.html.

Livingston, interview.

Ryne Nelson, "Kyrie Irving Wants to Start a 'Self-Sustaining Community,'" *Slam Magazine*, July 29, 2017, https://www.slamonline.com/archives/kyrie-irving-self-sustaining-community-ecovillage/#kujDMoCDEJj0Xaoc.97.

Nathaniel Friedman, "It's Kyrie Irving's World Now," *GQ*, January 17, 2018, https://www.gq.com/story/the-flat-world-of-kyrie-irving.

Friedman, "It's Kyrie Irving's World Now."

Sopan Deb, "Kyrie Irving Doesn't Know if the Earth Is Round or Flat. He Does Want to Discuss It," *New York Times*, June 8, 2018, https://www.nytimes.com/2018/06/08/movies/kyrie-irving-nba-celtics-earth.html.

Jason Owens, "Kyrie Irving, Nike Double Down on Spreading Flat-Earth Ignorance," January 2, 2018, Yahoo! Sports. https://sports.yahoo.com/kyrie-irving-nike-double-spreading-flat-earth-ignorance-043319683.html.

Joseph, "Kyrie Irving Apologized for Saying Earth Is Flat," *USA Today*, October 1, 2018, https://www.usatoday.com/story/sports/ftw/2018/10/01/kyrie-irving-apologized-for-saying-the-earth-is-flat-i-was-huge-into-conspiracies/38012367/.

14. THE GREAT ESCAPE

Jeff Schudel, "LeBron James Taking Credit for Kyrie Irving's Success," *News-Herald*, September 30, 2017, https://www.news-herald.com/sports/lebron-james-taking-credit-for-kyrie-irving-s-success-jeff/article_b98f9669-8a57-5e3d-a888-955a42644409.html.

MacMullan, "Behind Kyrie Irving's Controversial Departure."

MacMullan, "Behind Kyrie Irving's Controversial Departure."

Jared Weiss, "Former Cavs GM David Griffin Details Kyrie Irving's Trade Request and Its Root Cause," Celtics Wire, November 14, 2017, https://celticswire.usatoday.com/2017/11/14/david-griffin-kyrie-irving-cleveland-cavaliers-trade-boston-celtics-lebron-james-isaiah-thomas/.

Windhorst, "LeBron James: Doubt of Cavs' Potential Crept in Midseason," ESPN, May 31, 2018, http://www.espn.com/nba/story/_/id/23654249/lebron-james-faith -cleveland-cavaliers-shaken-midseason.

Bill Simmons, "David Griffin on How the NBA's Batman-and-Robin Effect Broke up Kyrie Irving and LeBron James," The Ringer, May 9, 2018, https://www.theringer .com/the-bill-simmons-podcast/2018/5/9/17337792/david-griffin-bill-simmons -podcast-kyrie-irving-lebron-james.

MacMullan, "Behind Kyrie Irving's Controversial Departure."

Chris Chavez, "Kyrie Irving Didn't Tell LeBron James He Wanted to Leave Cleveland, Doesn't Care Now," *Sports Illustrated*, September 18, 2017, https://www.si.com /nba/2017/09/18/kyrie-irving-first-take-lebron-james-trade-stephen-smith.

15. SPEAKING AND SAYING NOTHING

Brady Klopfer, email interview with author, October 31, 2018.

Dan Feldman, "Kyrie Irving's Reported Preferred Trade Destinations: Knicks, Heat, Spurs, Timberwolves," NBC Sports, July 21, 2017, https://nba.nbcsports.com/2017 /07/21/kyrie-irvings-reported-preferred-trade-destinations-knicks-heat-spurs -timberwolves/.

Dan Steinberg, "Kyrie Irving Really Wasn't Buying What 'First Take' Was Selling," *Washington Post*, September 19, 2017, https://www.washingtonpost.com/.

Chavez, "Kyrie Irving Didn't tell LeBron."

Steinberg, "Kyrie Irving Really Wasn't Buying."

Jonathan Sherman, "ESPN Analyst Slams Kyrie Irving for Contradicting Himself Several Times on 'First Take,'" Cavaliers Nation, September 19, 2017, https:// cavaliersnation.com/2017/09/19/espn-analyst-slams-kyrie-irving-for-contradicting -himself-several-times-on-first-take/.

Chavez, "Kyrie Irving Didn't Tell LeBron."

Livingston, interview.

Chris Forsberg and Brian Windhorst, "LeBron James Opens Up about Kyrie Irving's Decision to Leave Cavaliers," ESPN, September 25, 2017, http://www.espn.com/nba /story/_/id/20818619/lebron-james-opens-kyrie-irving-decision-leave-cavaliers.

16. GOING GREEN

Forsberg, "'It Was Just an Energy Shift: A Weird Week of Waiting for Kyrie and Boston,'" ESPN, August 30, 2018, http://www.espn.com/nba/story/_/id/24505385 /inside-week-uncertainty-kyrie-irving-officially-became-boston-celtic-nba.

Chavez, "Kyrie Irving Didn't Tell LeBron."

Jay King, "Kyrie Irving, Dominating in Crunch-Time, Compares Boston Celtics Coach Brad Stevens to Driving School Teacher," Mass Live, November 19, 2017,

https://www.masslive.com/celtics/index.ssf/2017/11/kyrie_irving_dominating
_in_cru.html.

King, "Kyrie Irving, Dominating in Crunch-Time."

Forsberg, "Kyrie Irving and the Celtics Are Flat-Out Dominating on Defense," ESPN,
November 8, 2017, http://www.espn.com/nba/story/_/id/21329484/kyrie-irving
-boston-celtics-flat-dominating-defense.

Dan Shaughnessy, "Kyrie Irving Makes All the Difference," *Boston Globe*, December
3, 2017, https://www.bostonglobe.com/sports/celtics/2017/12/02/kyrie-irving
-makes-all-difference/IsERPe2Q5eh6lLbGJFP5FO/story.html.

Shaughnessy, "Kyrie Irving Makes All the Difference."

Liam O'Brien, "Kyrie Irving's Recent Defensive Struggles Hurting Celtics," Hardwood
Houdini. December 20, 2017, https://hardwoodhoudini.com/2017/12/20/kyrie
-irvings-recent-defensive-struggles-hurting-celtics/.

Klopfer, interview.

2017–18 NBA Player Stats: Advanced, Basketball Reference, https://www.basketball
-reference.com/leagues/NBA_2018_advanced.html.

Nik DeCosta-Klipa and Nicole Yang, "How Kyrie Irving's Knee Problems Started
and What They Mean for the Celtics," Boston.com, March 26, 2018, https://www
.boston.com/sports/boston-celtics/2018/03/26/kyrie-irving-knee-injury-surgery
-update.

Kyle Hightower, "Kyrie Irving Out Remainder of Season after Surgery Reveals Infection," NBA.com, April 5, 2018, http://www.nba.com/article/2018/04/05/boston
-celtics-kyrie-irving-out-remainder-season-left-knee.

17. A QUESTION OF VALUE

Kevin Pelton, "How Far Can the Celtics Go in the Playoffs without Kyrie?" ESPN,
April 5, 2018, http://www.espn.com/nba/story/_/id/23040426/can-boston-celtics
-make-deep-playoff-run-kyrie-irving-nba.

Andrew Sharp, "Waiting on Answers to All the Best Kyrie Irving Questions," *Sports
Illustrated*, May 23, 2018, https://www.si.com/nba/2018/05/23/nba-playoffs-kyrie
-irving-celtics-cavaliers-eastern-conference-finals.

Westerholm, "Boston Celtics vs. Cleveland Cavaliers: Kyrie Irving's Absence Looms
over Both Teams Prior to ECF," Mass Live, May 13, 2018, https://www.masslive
.com/celtics/index.ssf/2018/05/boston_celtics_vs_cleveland_ca_20.html.

Joshua Schrock, "Are Celtics Better without Gordon Hayward, Kyrie Irving? Danny
Ainge Scoffs at Idea," NESN, May 28, 2018, https://nesn.com/2018/05/are-celtics
-better-without-kyrie-irving-gordon-hayward-danny-ainge-scoffs-at-idea/.

Adam Himmelsbach, "Kyrie Irving Had a Few Things to Say about LeBron, His Knee,
and Next Season," *Boston Globe*, June 12, 2018, https://www.bostonglobe.com

/sports/celtics/2018/06/12/kyrie-irving-noncommittal-about-possible-reunion-with-lebron-james/8Tl1FqJkYexPsqryN8Iv4M/story.html.

Deb, "Kyrie Irving Doesn't Know."

Deb, "Kyrie Irving Doesn't Know."

Jeff Zillgitt, "Kyrie Irving: 'Uncle Drew' Movie about Paying Homage to the Older Generations," *USA Today*, July 1, 2018, https://www.usatoday.com/story/sports/nba/2018/06/28/uncle-drew-movie-kyrie-irving/741488002/.

Zillgitt, "Kyrie Irving: 'Uncle Drew' Movie."

Nick Allen, "Uncle Drew." RogerEbert.com, June 29, 2018, https://www.rogerebert.com/reviews/uncle-drew-2018.

"Uncle Drew," Box Office Mojo, https://www.boxofficemojo.com/movies/?id=uncledrew.html.

18. A RECOVERY AND . . . A REUNION?

Himmelsbach, "Kyrie Irving Had a Few Things."

"Kyrie Irving: LeBron James 'Checks Every Mark' in MVP race," ESPN, June 27, 2018, http://www.espn.com/nba/story/_/id/23925622/kyrie-irving-boston-celtics.

Pete Blackburn, "Kyrie Irving Doesn't Sound Like He Definitely Wants to Leave the Celtics Next Summer: 'We're Pretty F'ing Good Here,'" CBS Sports, September 26, 2018, https://www.cbssports.com/nba/news/kyrie-irving-doesnt-sound-like-he-definitely-wants-to-leave-the-celtics-next-summer-were-pretty-fing-good-here/.

"Kyrie Irving Says He Plans on Re-Signing with Celtics," ESPN, October 5, 2018, http://www.espn.com/nba/story/_/id/24896082/kyrie-irving-says-plans-re-signing-celtics.

"Kyrie Irving Says He Plans."

Rick Bonnell, "Celtics' Kyrie Irving Says Goodbye to Cleveland, Hello to 'Real, Live Sports City,'" *Charlotte Observer*, October 11, 2017, https://www.charlotteobserver.com/sports/nba/charlotte-hornets/article178378341.html.

Ian Begley, "Kyrie Irving Has No Problem with Collin Sexton Wearing No. 2 for Cavs," ESPN, June 25, 2018, http://www.espn.com/nba/story/_/id/23903894/kyrie-irving-no-problem-collin-sexton-wearing-no-2-jersey-cleveland-cavaliers.

Westerholm, "Kyrie Irving's High School Coach." Kurt Helin, "Celtics GM Ainge on Kyrie Irving: 'He Can Be the Best Player in the World,'" NBC Sports, October 5, 2018, https://nba.nbcsports.com/2018/10/05/celtics-gm-ainge-on-kyrie-irving-he-can-be-the-best-player-in-the-world/.

EPILOGUE

Mark Murphy, "Kyrie Irving, Scuffling Celtics Hear it from Garden Crowd," *Boston Herald*, November 22, 2018, https://www.bostonherald.com/2018/11/22/kyrie-irving-scuffling-celtics-hear-it-from-garden-crowd/.

Tim Bontemps, "Kyrie Irving Says Call to LeBron James Was Needed 'to Move Forward,'" ESPN, February 20, 2019, http://www.espn.com/nba/story/_/id/26039461/kyrie-irving-says-call-lebron-james-needed-move-forward.

Index